The Urbana Free Library

To renew: call **217-367-4057**
or go to **urbanafreelibrary.org**
and select **My Account**

Magical History Tour

The Great Pyramid

FABRICE ERRE
Writer

SYLVAIN SAVOIA
Artist

New York

Magical History Tour

History Tour

#1 "The Great Pyramid"

By Fabrice Erre and Sylvain Savoia

Original series editors: Frédéric Niffle and Lewis Trondheim
Translation: Joseph Laredo
Lettering: Cromatik Ltd

Jeff Whitman – Managing Editor
Jim Salicrup
Editor-in-Chief

ISBN 978-1-5458-0633-3
© 2018 - DUPUIS - Erre - Savoia
Originally published in French as *"Le Fil de l'Histoire,
Tome 2 - La Pyramide de Khéops"*
All other material © 2021 Papercutz
www.papercutz.com

Papercutz books may be purchased for business or promotional use. For
information on bulk purchases please contact Macmillan Corporate and
Premium Sales Department at (800) 221-7945 x5442.

Printed in Malaysia
January 2021

Distributed by Macmillan
First Printing

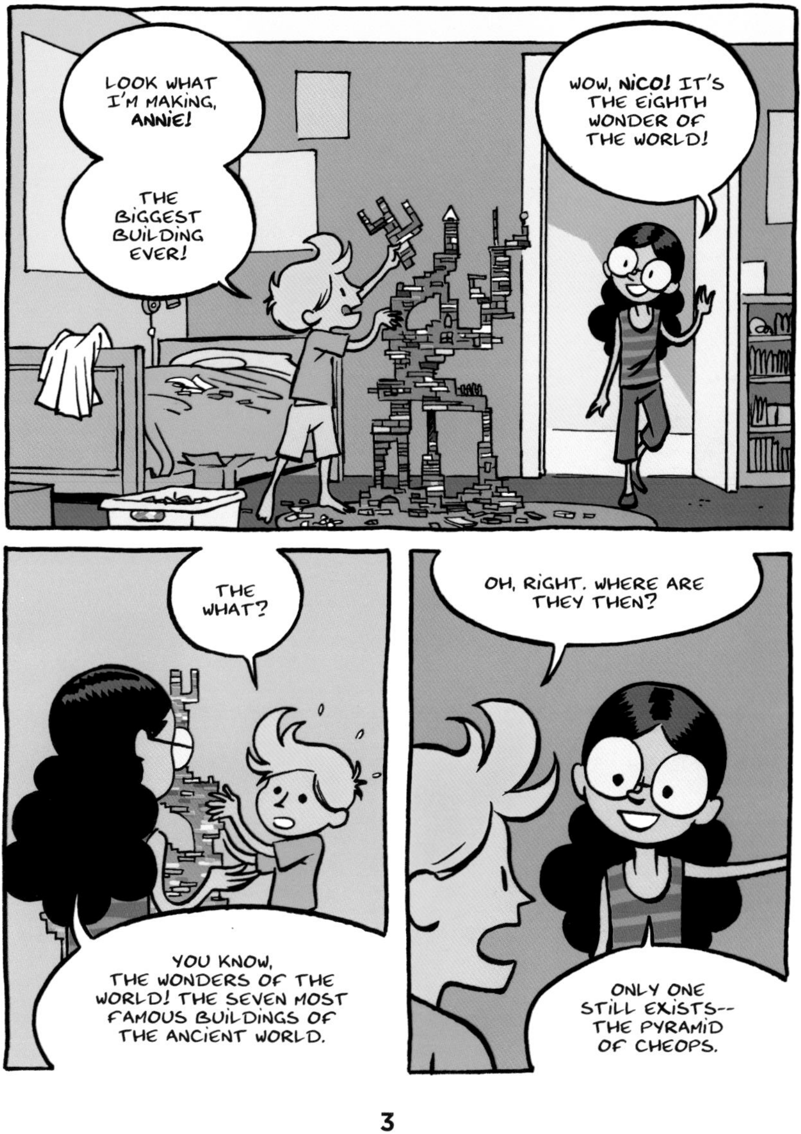
LOOK WHAT I'M MAKING, ANNIE!
THE BIGGEST BUILDING EVER!
WOW, NICO! IT'S THE EIGHTH WONDER OF THE WORLD!
THE WHAT?
YOU KNOW, THE WONDERS OF THE WORLD! THE SEVEN MOST FAMOUS BUILDINGS OF THE ANCIENT WORLD.
OH, RIGHT. WHERE ARE THEY THEN?
ONLY ONE STILL EXISTS-- THE PYRAMID OF CHEOPS.

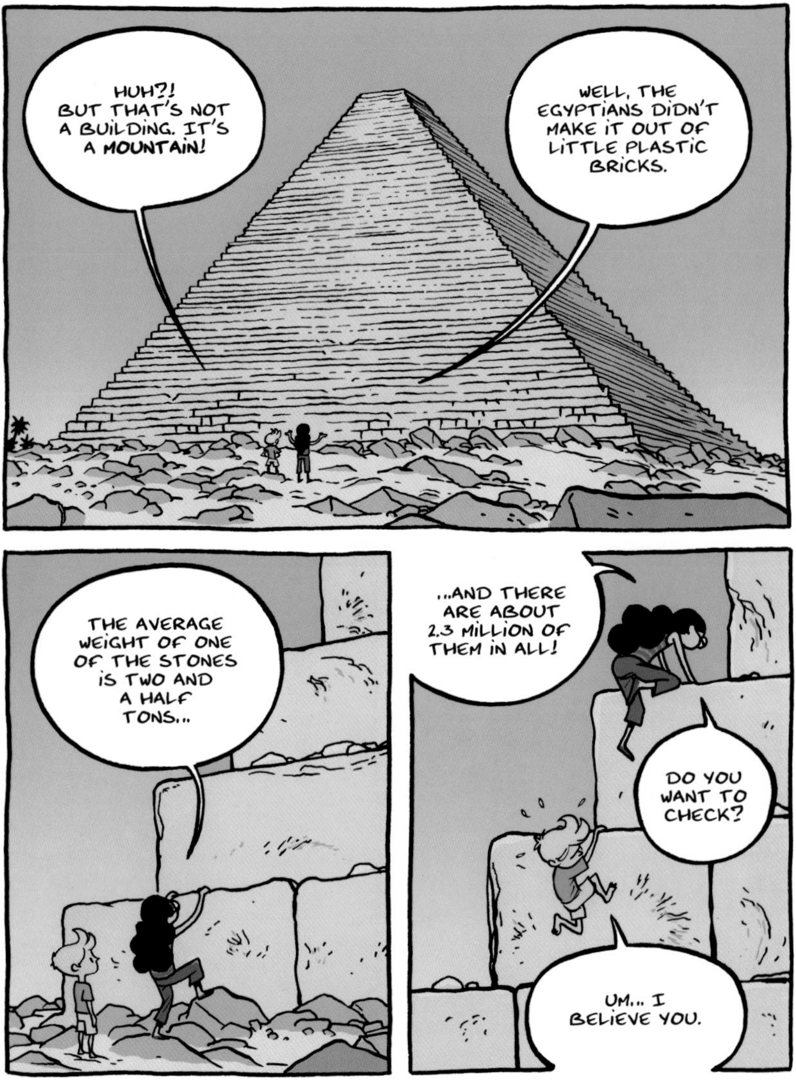
HUH?! BUT THAT'S NOT A BUILDING. IT'S A **MOUNTAIN**!
WELL, THE EGYPTIANS DIDN'T MAKE IT OUT OF LITTLE PLASTIC BRICKS.
THE AVERAGE WEIGHT OF ONE OF THE STONES IS TWO AND A HALF TONS...
...AND THERE ARE ABOUT 2.3 MILLION OF THEM IN ALL!
DO YOU WANT TO CHECK?
UM... I BELIEVE YOU.

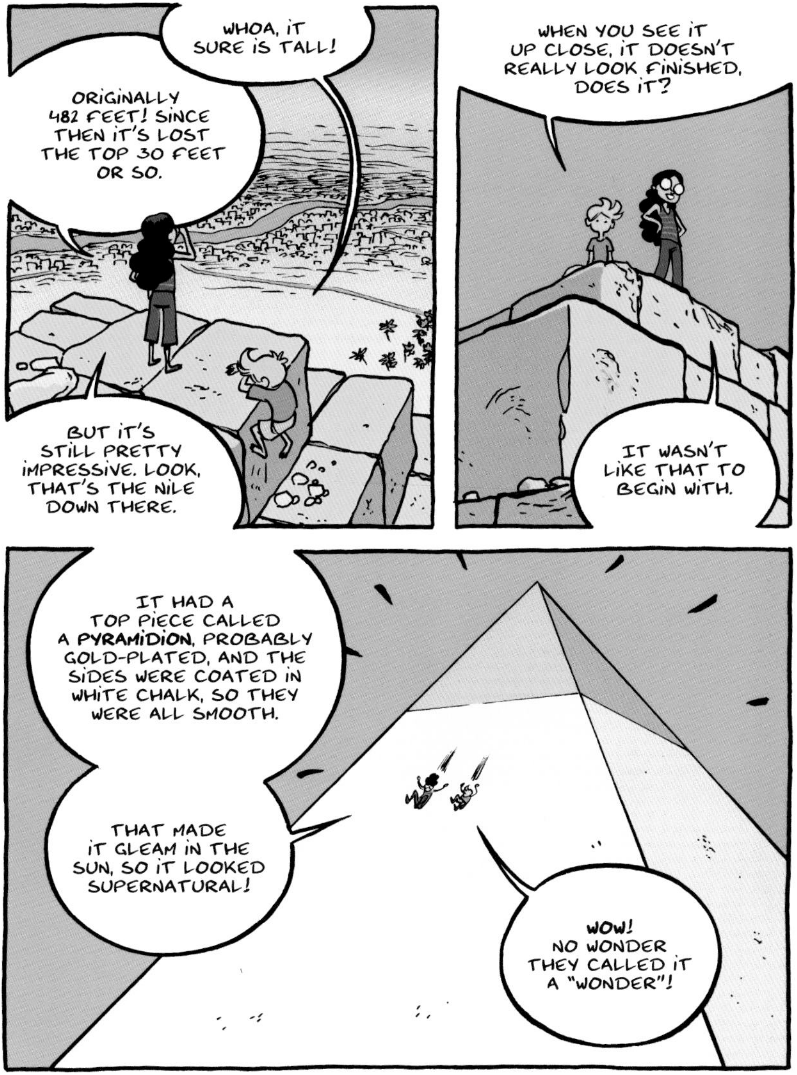
WHOA, IT SURE IS TALL!
ORIGINALLY 482 FEET! SINCE THEN IT'S LOST THE TOP 30 FEET OR SO.
BUT IT'S STILL PRETTY IMPRESSIVE. LOOK, THAT'S THE NILE DOWN THERE.
WHEN YOU SEE IT UP CLOSE, IT DOESN'T REALLY LOOK FINISHED, DOES IT?
IT WASN'T LIKE THAT TO BEGIN WITH.
IT HAD A TOP PIECE CALLED A **PYRAMIDION**, PROBABLY GOLD-PLATED, AND THE SIDES WERE COATED IN WHITE CHALK, SO THEY WERE ALL SMOOTH.
THAT MADE IT GLEAM IN THE SUN, SO IT LOOKED SUPERNATURAL!
WOW! NO WONDER THEY CALLED IT A "WONDER"!

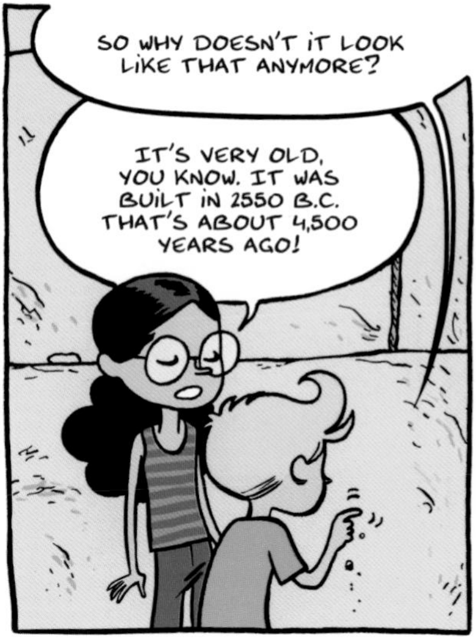
SO WHY DOESN'T IT LOOK LIKE THAT ANYMORE?
IT'S VERY OLD, YOU KNOW. IT WAS BUILT IN 2550 B.C. THAT'S ABOUT 4,500 YEARS AGO!

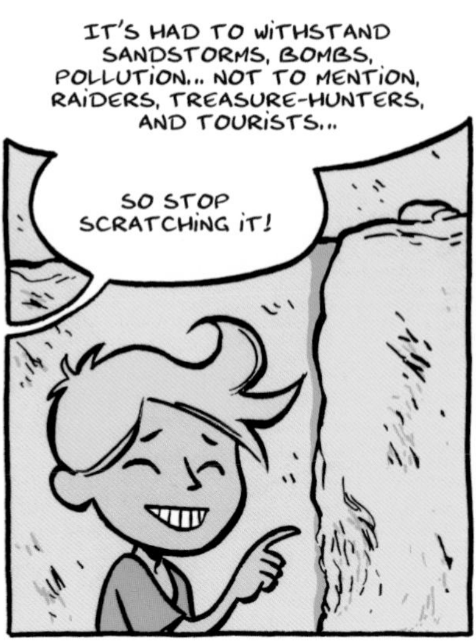
IT'S HAD TO WITHSTAND SANDSTORMS, BOMBS, POLLUTION... NOT TO MENTION, RAIDERS, TREASURE-HUNTERS, AND TOURISTS...
SO STOP SCRATCHING IT!

FOR NEARLY 4,000 YEARS, IT WAS THE TALLEST BUILDING IN THE WORLD. IT WAS THE FIRST OF THE SEVEN WONDERS OF THE WORLD TO BE BUILT AND TODAY IT'S THE ONLY ONE STILL STANDING!

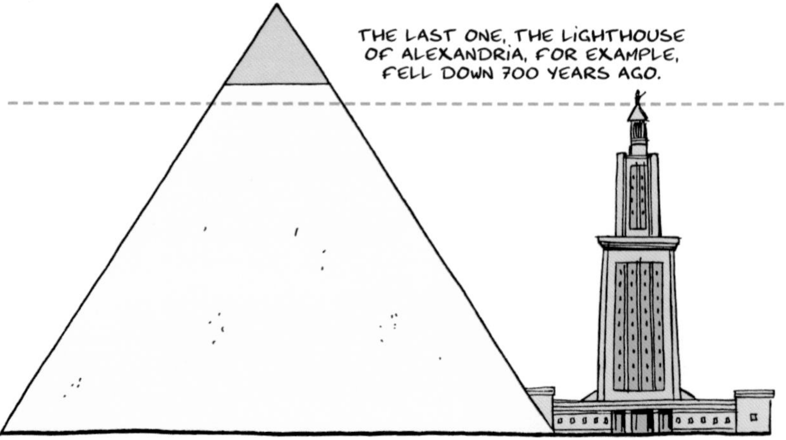
THE LAST ONE, THE LIGHTHOUSE OF ALEXANDRIA, FOR EXAMPLE, FELL DOWN 700 YEARS AGO.

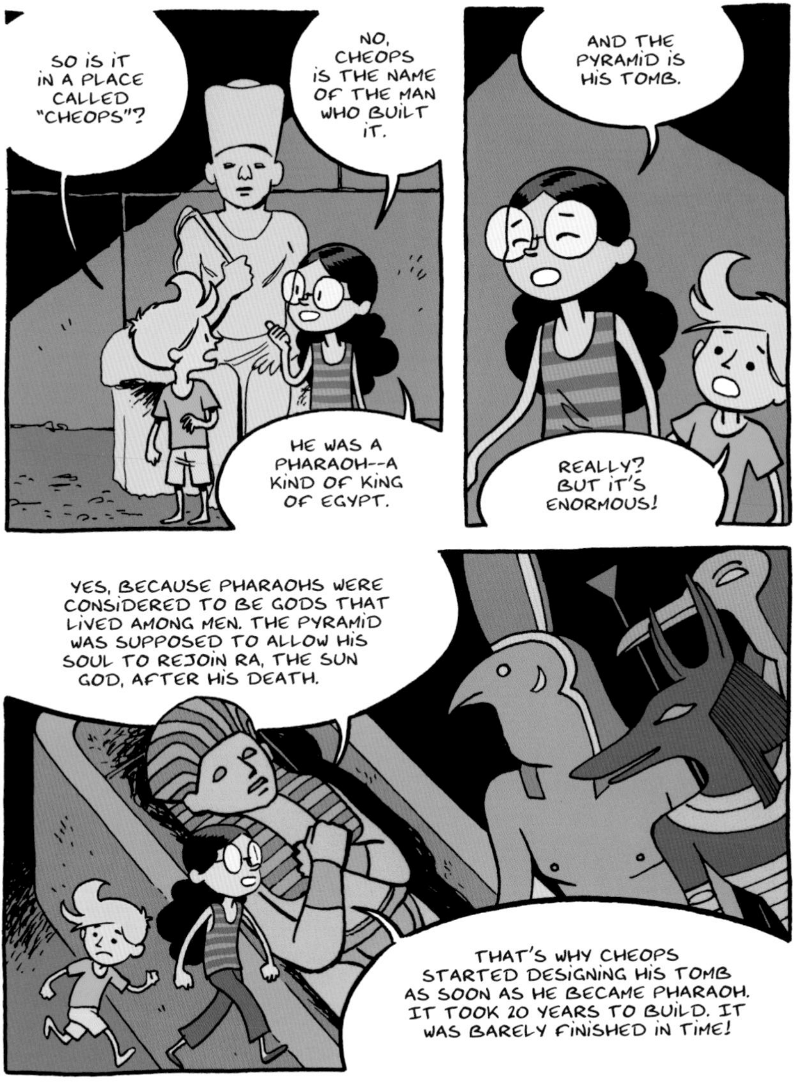
SO IS IT IN A PLACE CALLED "CHEOPS"?
NO, CHEOPS IS THE NAME OF THE MAN WHO BUILT IT.
HE WAS A PHARAOH--A KIND OF KING OF EGYPT.
AND THE PYRAMID IS HIS TOMB.
REALLY? BUT IT'S ENORMOUS!
YES, BECAUSE PHARAOHS WERE CONSIDERED TO BE GODS THAT LIVED AMONG MEN. THE PYRAMID WAS SUPPOSED TO ALLOW HIS SOUL TO REJOIN RA, THE SUN GOD, AFTER HIS DEATH.
THAT'S WHY CHEOPS STARTED DESIGNING HIS TOMB AS SOON AS HE BECAME PHARAOH. IT TOOK 20 YEARS TO BUILD. IT WAS BARELY FINISHED IN TIME!

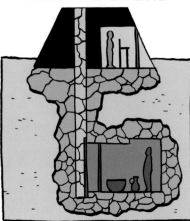

SO DID ALL THE PHARAOHS MAKE PYRAMIDS?

NO, BUT CHEOPS WASN'T THE FIRST TO BUILD ONE.

THE EARLY PHARAOHS WERE BURIED UNDERGROUND, WITH THEIR STATUE IN A BUILDING CALLED A MASTABA ABOVE.

THEN, 100 YEARS OR SO BEFORE CHEOPS, PHARAOH DJOSER'S ARCHITECT, IMHOTEP, THOUGHT OF STACKING MASTABAS ONE ON TOP OF THE OTHER--AND MADE THE FIRST STEPPED PYRAMID.

OH, SO YOU COULD SAY THE PYRAMIDS "GREW"!

AFTER THAT, IT BECAME KIND OF A FAMILY BUSINESS. CHEOPS'S FATHER, SNEFERU, DECIDED TO OUTDO THE OTHERS AND BUILD A SMOOTH-SIDED PYRAMID...

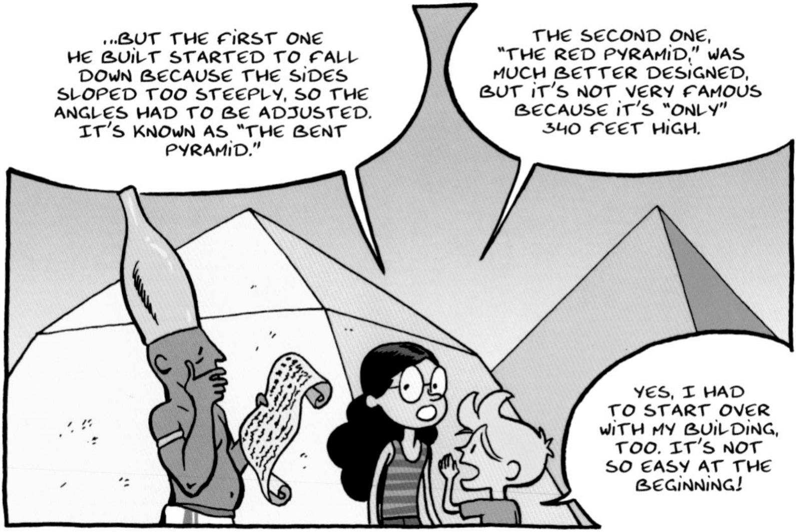
...BUT THE FIRST ONE HE BUILT STARTED TO FALL DOWN BECAUSE THE SIDES SLOPED TOO STEEPLY, SO THE ANGLES HAD TO BE ADJUSTED. IT'S KNOWN AS "THE BENT PYRAMID."
THE SECOND ONE, "THE RED PYRAMID," WAS MUCH BETTER DESIGNED, BUT IT'S NOT VERY FAMOUS BECAUSE IT'S "ONLY" 340 FEET HIGH.
YES, I HAD TO START OVER WITH MY BUILDING, TOO. IT'S NOT SO EASY AT THE BEGINNING!

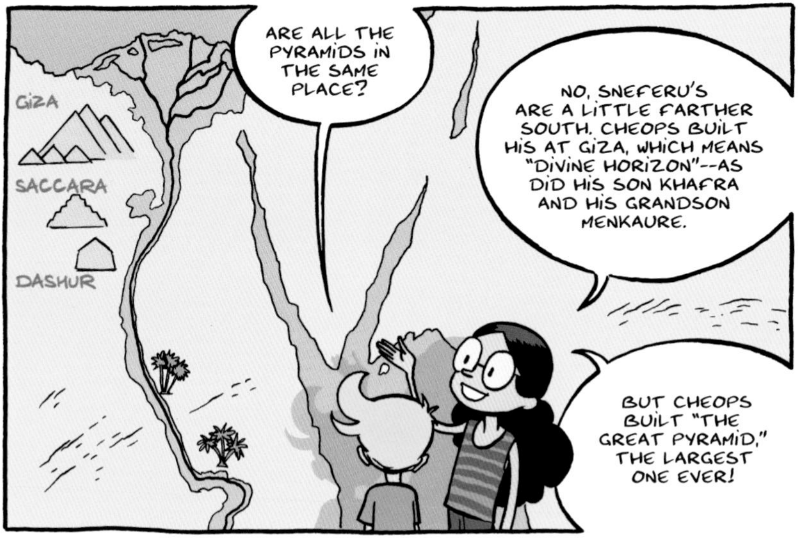
ARE ALL THE PYRAMIDS IN THE SAME PLACE?
GIZA
SACCARA
DASHUR
NO, SNEFERU'S ARE A LITTLE FARTHER SOUTH. CHEOPS BUILT HIS AT GIZA, WHICH MEANS "DIVINE HORIZON"--AS DID HIS SON KHAFRA AND HIS GRANDSON MENKAURE.
BUT CHEOPS BUILT "THE GREAT PYRAMID," THE LARGEST ONE EVER!

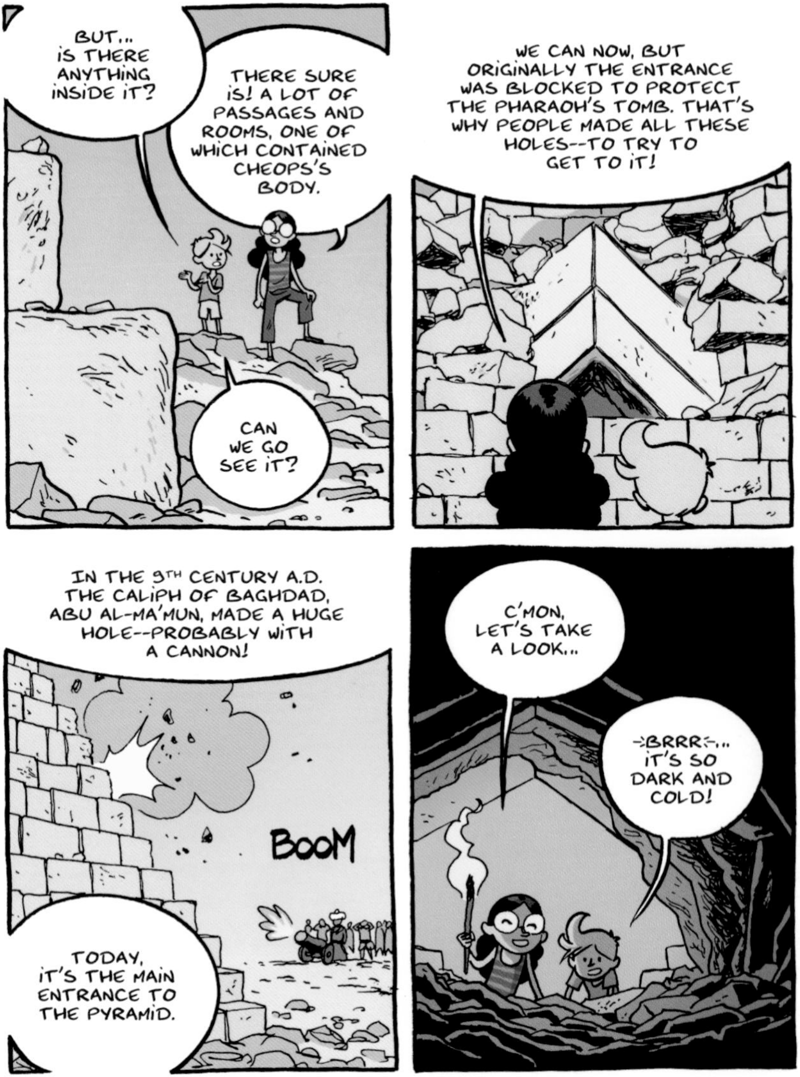
BUT... IS THERE ANYTHING INSIDE IT?
THERE SURE IS! A LOT OF PASSAGES AND ROOMS, ONE OF WHICH CONTAINED CHEOPS'S BODY.
CAN WE GO SEE IT?
WE CAN NOW, BUT ORIGINALLY THE ENTRANCE WAS BLOCKED TO PROTECT THE PHARAOH'S TOMB. THAT'S WHY PEOPLE MADE ALL THESE HOLES--TO TRY TO GET TO IT!
IN THE 9TH CENTURY A.D. THE CALIPH OF BAGHDAD, ABU AL-MA'MUN, MADE A HUGE HOLE--PROBABLY WITH A CANNON!
BOOM
TODAY, IT'S THE MAIN ENTRANCE TO THE PYRAMID.
C'MON, LET'S TAKE A LOOK...
BRRR... IT'S SO DARK AND COLD!

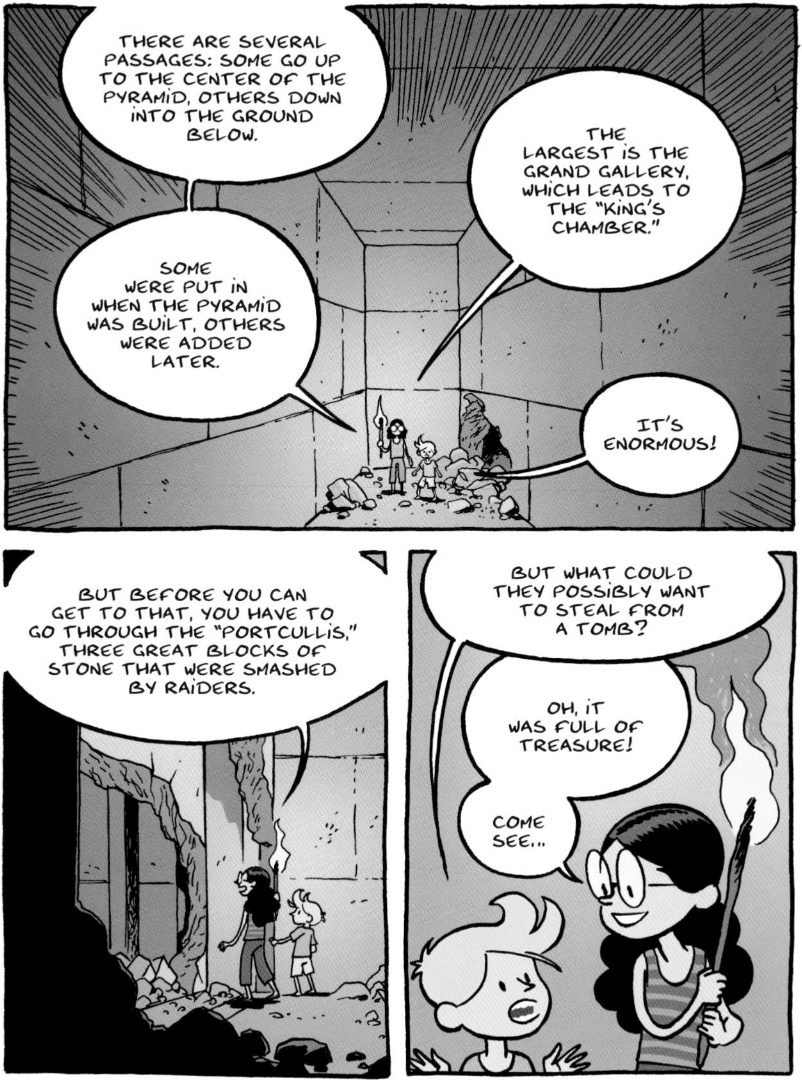
THERE ARE SEVERAL PASSAGES: SOME GO UP TO THE CENTER OF THE PYRAMID, OTHERS DOWN INTO THE GROUND BELOW.
SOME WERE PUT IN WHEN THE PYRAMID WAS BUILT, OTHERS WERE ADDED LATER.
THE LARGEST IS THE GRAND GALLERY, WHICH LEADS TO THE "KING'S CHAMBER."
IT'S ENORMOUS!
BUT BEFORE YOU CAN GET TO THAT, YOU HAVE TO GO THROUGH THE "PORTCULLIS," THREE GREAT BLOCKS OF STONE THAT WERE SMASHED BY RAIDERS.
BUT WHAT COULD THEY POSSIBLY WANT TO STEAL FROM A TOMB?
OH, IT WAS FULL OF TREASURE!
COME SEE...

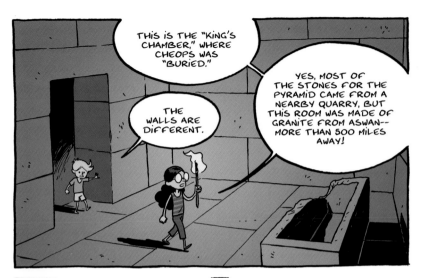

THIS IS THE "KING'S CHAMBER," WHERE CHEOPS WAS "BURIED."

THE WALLS ARE DIFFERENT.

YES, MOST OF THE STONES FOR THE PYRAMID CAME FROM A NEARBY QUARRY, BUT THIS ROOM WAS MADE OF GRANITE FROM ASWAN-- MORE THAN 500 MILES AWAY!

AND THIS IS THE SARCOPHAGUS-- THE PHARAOH'S ACTUAL TOMB.

IT'S ALL SO GLOOMY...

BACK THEN IT WAS REALLY DIFFERENT. ALL KINDS OF THINGS WERE LEFT IN THE ROOM TO ACCOMPANY THE PHARAOH TO THE NEXT LIFE.

THERE WERE CLOTHES AND JEWELRY--EVEN FOOD!

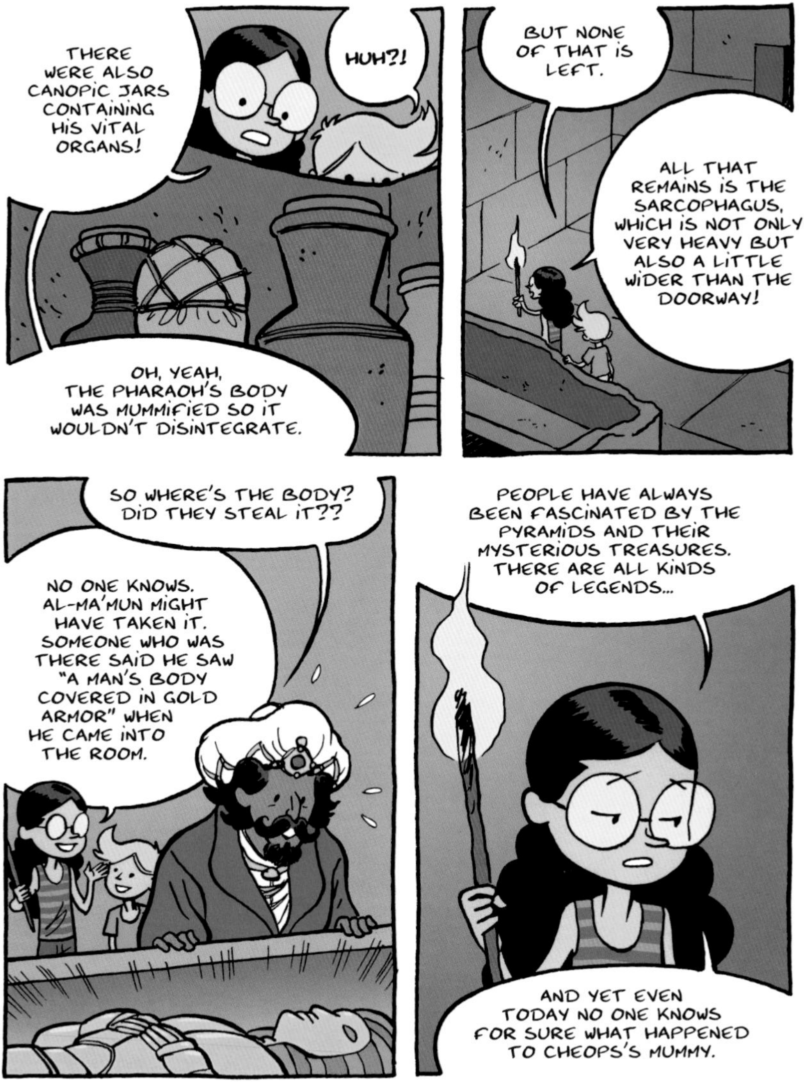
THERE WERE ALSO CANOPIC JARS CONTAINING HIS VITAL ORGANS!
HUH?!
OH, YEAH, THE PHARAOH'S BODY WAS MUMMIFIED SO IT WOULDN'T DISINTEGRATE.
BUT NONE OF THAT IS LEFT.
ALL THAT REMAINS IS THE SARCOPHAGUS, WHICH IS NOT ONLY VERY HEAVY BUT ALSO A LITTLE WIDER THAN THE DOORWAY!
SO WHERE'S THE BODY? DID THEY STEAL IT??
NO ONE KNOWS. AL-MA'MUN MIGHT HAVE TAKEN IT. SOMEONE WHO WAS THERE SAID HE SAW "A MAN'S BODY COVERED IN GOLD ARMOR" WHEN HE CAME INTO THE ROOM.
PEOPLE HAVE ALWAYS BEEN FASCINATED BY THE PYRAMIDS AND THEIR MYSTERIOUS TREASURES. THERE ARE ALL KINDS OF LEGENDS...
AND YET EVEN TODAY NO ONE KNOWS FOR SURE WHAT HAPPENED TO CHEOPS'S MUMMY.

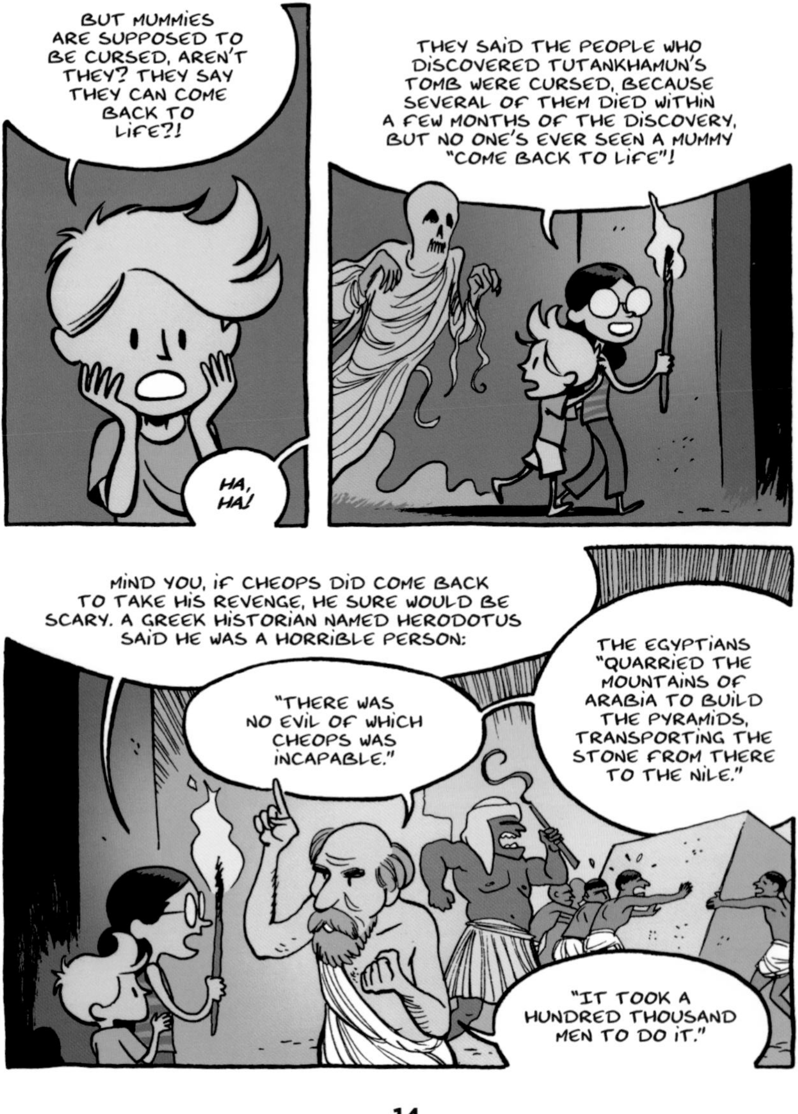
BUT MUMMIES ARE SUPPOSED TO BE CURSED, AREN'T THEY? THEY SAY THEY CAN COME BACK TO LIFE?!
HA, HA!
THEY SAID THE PEOPLE WHO DISCOVERED TUTANKHAMUN'S TOMB WERE CURSED, BECAUSE SEVERAL OF THEM DIED WITHIN A FEW MONTHS OF THE DISCOVERY, BUT NO ONE'S EVER SEEN A MUMMY "COME BACK TO LIFE"!
MIND YOU, IF CHEOPS DID COME BACK TO TAKE HIS REVENGE, HE SURE WOULD BE SCARY. A GREEK HISTORIAN NAMED HERODOTUS SAID HE WAS A HORRIBLE PERSON:
"THERE WAS NO EVIL OF WHICH CHEOPS WAS INCAPABLE."
THE EGYPTIANS "QUARRIED THE MOUNTAINS OF ARABIA TO BUILD THE PYRAMIDS, TRANSPORTING THE STONE FROM THERE TO THE NILE."
"IT TOOK A HUNDRED THOUSAND MEN TO DO IT."

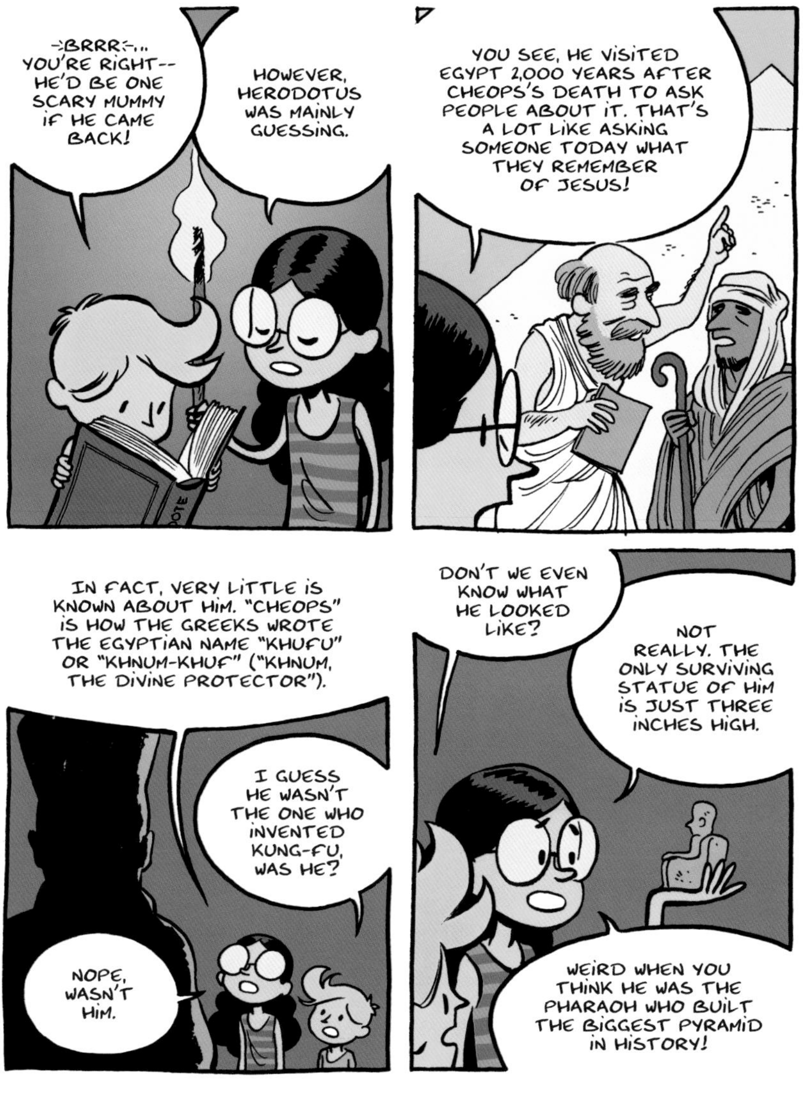
⇢BRRR⇠... YOU'RE RIGHT-- HE'D BE ONE SCARY MUMMY IF HE CAME BACK!
HOWEVER, HERODOTUS WAS MAINLY GUESSING.
YOU SEE, HE VISITED EGYPT 2,000 YEARS AFTER CHEOPS'S DEATH TO ASK PEOPLE ABOUT IT. THAT'S A LOT LIKE ASKING SOMEONE TODAY WHAT THEY REMEMBER OF JESUS!
IN FACT, VERY LITTLE IS KNOWN ABOUT HIM. "CHEOPS" IS HOW THE GREEKS WROTE THE EGYPTIAN NAME "KHUFU" OR "KHNUM-KHUF" ("KHNUM, THE DIVINE PROTECTOR").
I GUESS HE WASN'T THE ONE WHO INVENTED KUNG-FU, WAS HE?
NOPE, WASN'T HIM.
DON'T WE EVEN KNOW WHAT HE LOOKED LIKE?
NOT REALLY. THE ONLY SURVIVING STATUE OF HIM IS JUST THREE INCHES HIGH.
WEIRD WHEN YOU THINK HE WAS THE PHARAOH WHO BUILT THE BIGGEST PYRAMID IN HISTORY!

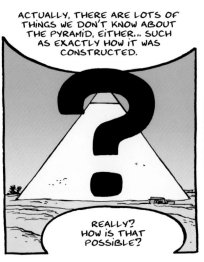

ACTUALLY, THERE ARE LOTS OF THINGS WE DON'T KNOW ABOUT THE PYRAMID, EITHER... SUCH AS EXACTLY HOW IT WAS CONSTRUCTED.

REALLY? HOW IS THAT POSSIBLE?

THERE'S NO RECORD OF IT, AND NO HIEROGLYPHICS THAT SHOW HOW IT WAS BUILT. IN FACT, THERE AREN'T ANY AT ALL ON THE PYRAMID ITSELF...

...APART FROM THE SYMBOL FOR "CHEOPS."

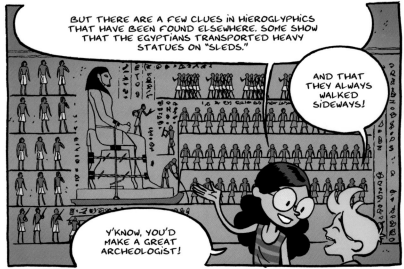

BUT THERE ARE A FEW CLUES IN HIEROGLYPHICS THAT HAVE BEEN FOUND ELSEWHERE. SOME SHOW THAT THE EGYPTIANS TRANSPORTED HEAVY STATUES ON "SLEDS."

AND THAT THEY ALWAYS WALKED SIDEWAYS!

Y'KNOW, YOU'D MAKE A GREAT ARCHEOLOGIST!

16

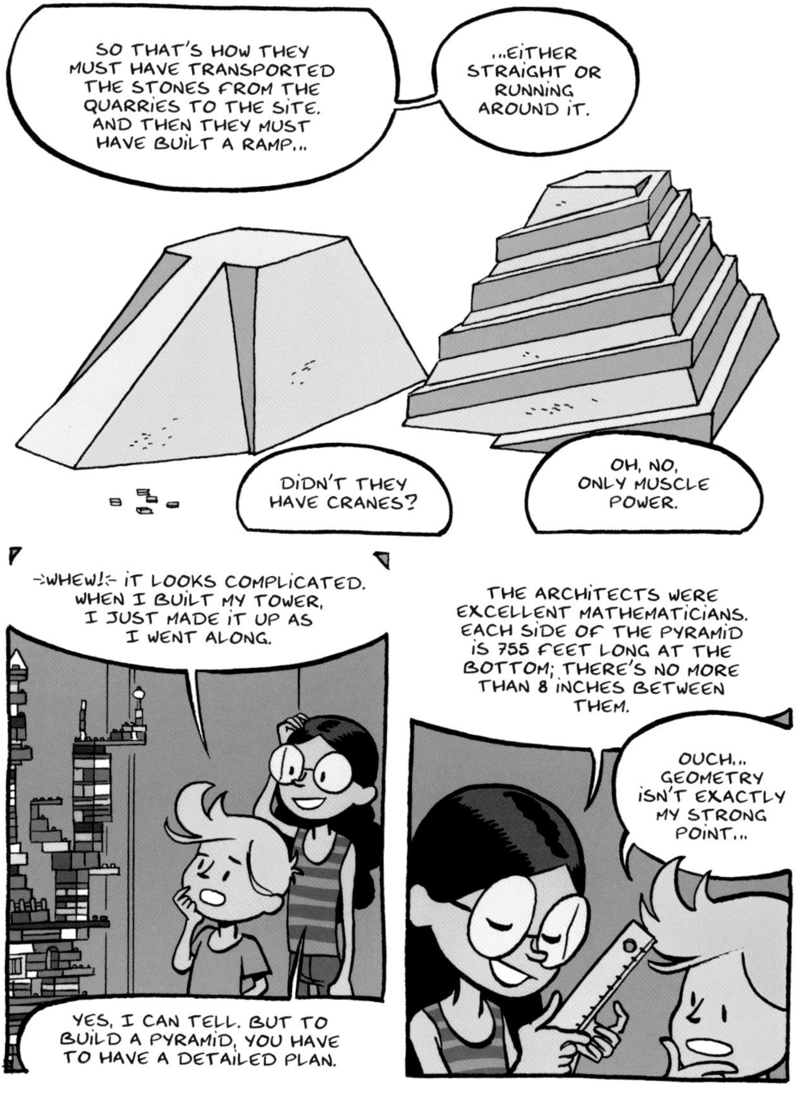

SO THAT'S HOW THEY MUST HAVE TRANSPORTED THE STONES FROM THE QUARRIES TO THE SITE. AND THEN THEY MUST HAVE BUILT A RAMP...
...EITHER STRAIGHT OR RUNNING AROUND IT.
DIDN'T THEY HAVE CRANES?
OH, NO, ONLY MUSCLE POWER.
WHEW! IT LOOKS COMPLICATED. WHEN I BUILT MY TOWER, I JUST MADE IT UP AS I WENT ALONG.
YES, I CAN TELL. BUT TO BUILD A PYRAMID, YOU HAVE TO HAVE A DETAILED PLAN.
THE ARCHITECTS WERE EXCELLENT MATHEMATICIANS. EACH SIDE OF THE PYRAMID IS 755 FEET LONG AT THE BOTTOM; THERE'S NO MORE THAN 8 INCHES BETWEEN THEM.
OUCH... GEOMETRY ISN'T EXACTLY MY STRONG POINT...

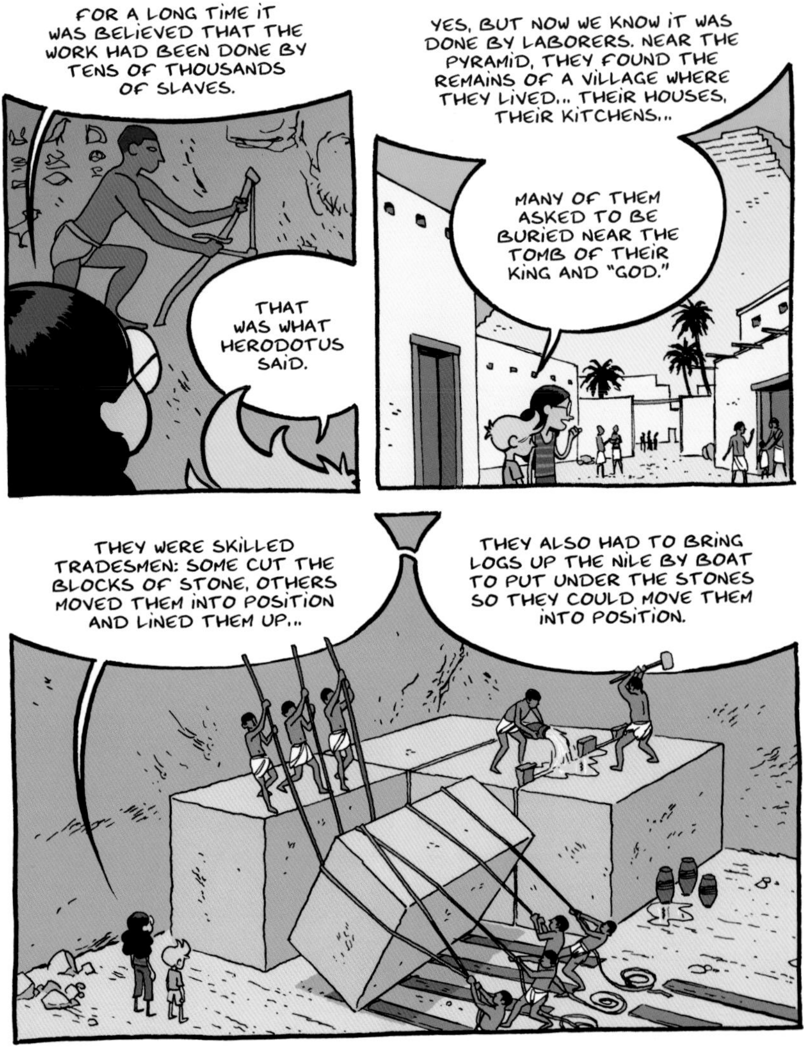
FOR A LONG TIME IT WAS BELIEVED THAT THE WORK HAD BEEN DONE BY TENS OF THOUSANDS OF SLAVES.
THAT WAS WHAT HERODOTUS SAID.
YES, BUT NOW WE KNOW IT WAS DONE BY LABORERS. NEAR THE PYRAMID, THEY FOUND THE REMAINS OF A VILLAGE WHERE THEY LIVED... THEIR HOUSES, THEIR KITCHENS...
MANY OF THEM ASKED TO BE BURIED NEAR THE TOMB OF THEIR KING AND "GOD."
THEY WERE SKILLED TRADESMEN: SOME CUT THE BLOCKS OF STONE, OTHERS MOVED THEM INTO POSITION AND LINED THEM UP...
THEY ALSO HAD TO BRING LOGS UP THE NILE BY BOAT TO PUT UNDER THE STONES SO THEY COULD MOVE THEM INTO POSITION.

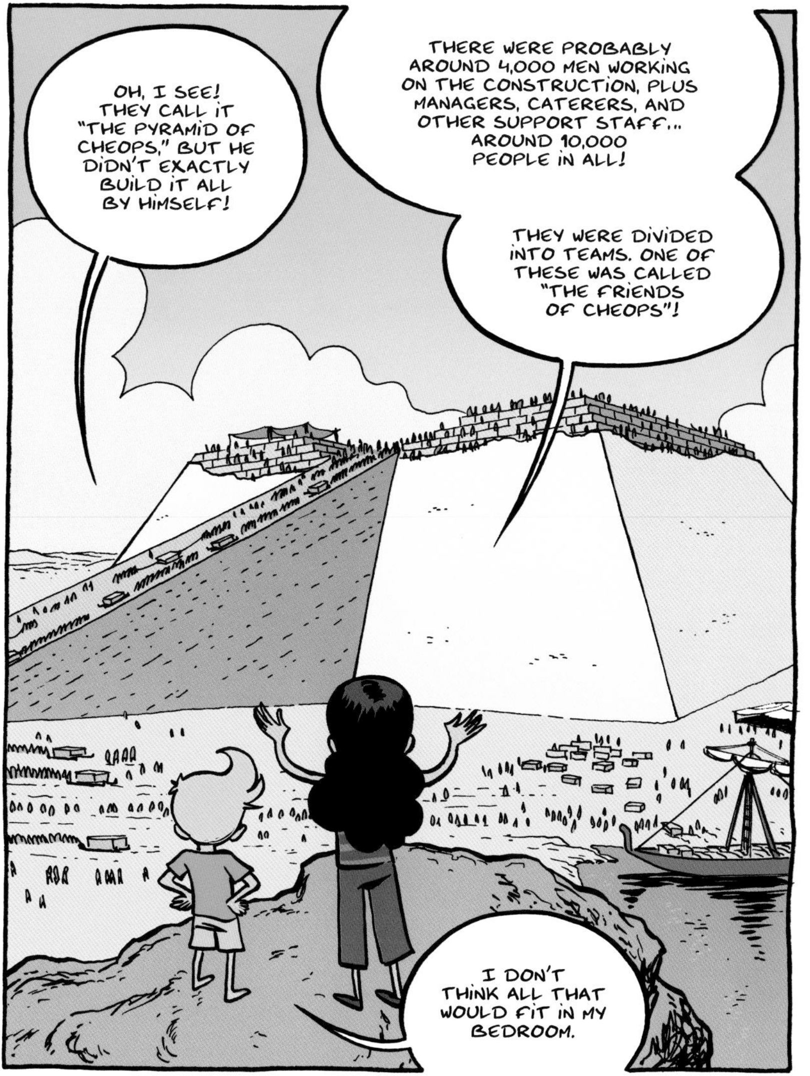
OH, I SEE! THEY CALL IT "THE PYRAMID OF CHEOPS," BUT HE DIDN'T EXACTLY BUILD IT ALL BY HIMSELF!
THERE WERE PROBABLY AROUND 4,000 MEN WORKING ON THE CONSTRUCTION, PLUS MANAGERS, CATERERS, AND OTHER SUPPORT STAFF... AROUND 10,000 PEOPLE IN ALL!
THEY WERE DIVIDED INTO TEAMS. ONE OF THESE WAS CALLED "THE FRIENDS OF CHEOPS"!
I DON'T THINK ALL THAT WOULD FIT IN MY BEDROOM.

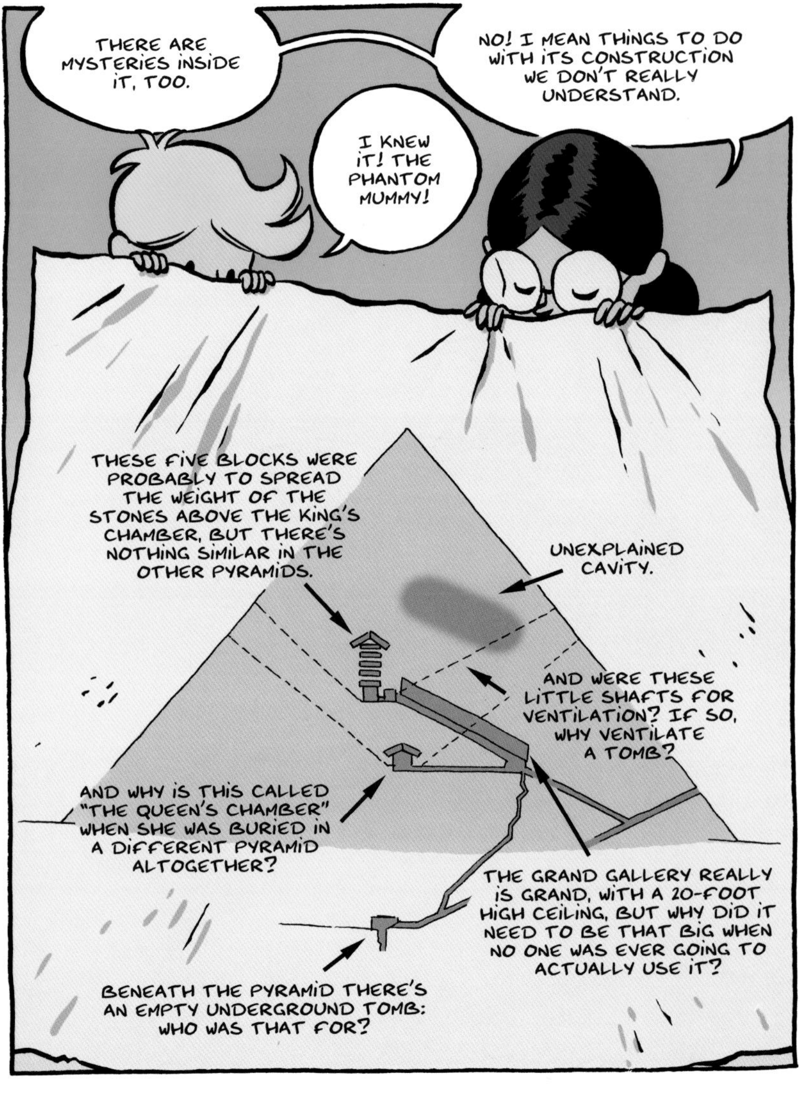
THERE ARE MYSTERIES INSIDE IT, TOO.
I KNEW IT! THE PHANTOM MUMMY!
NO! I MEAN THINGS TO DO WITH ITS CONSTRUCTION WE DON'T REALLY UNDERSTAND.
THESE FIVE BLOCKS WERE PROBABLY TO SPREAD THE WEIGHT OF THE STONES ABOVE THE KING'S CHAMBER, BUT THERE'S NOTHING SIMILAR IN THE OTHER PYRAMIDS.
UNEXPLAINED CAVITY.
AND WERE THESE LITTLE SHAFTS FOR VENTILATION? IF SO, WHY VENTILATE A TOMB?
AND WHY IS THIS CALLED "THE QUEEN'S CHAMBER" WHEN SHE WAS BURIED IN A DIFFERENT PYRAMID ALTOGETHER?
THE GRAND GALLERY REALLY IS GRAND, WITH A 20-FOOT HIGH CEILING, BUT WHY DID IT NEED TO BE THAT BIG WHEN NO ONE WAS EVER GOING TO ACTUALLY USE IT?
BENEATH THE PYRAMID THERE'S AN EMPTY UNDERGROUND TOMB: WHO WAS THAT FOR?

AND THERE ARE PROBABLY OTHER HIDDEN ROOMS!

FULL OF TREASURE?

MAYBE! BUT NO ONE'S ALLOWED TO REMOVE ANY MORE STONES FROM THE PYRAMID. IT'S SUFFERED ENOUGH ALREADY!

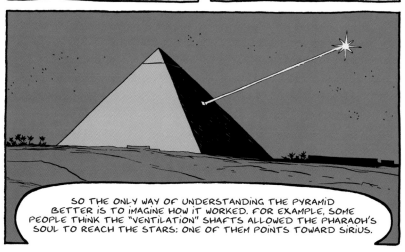

SO THE ONLY WAY OF UNDERSTANDING THE PYRAMID BETTER IS TO IMAGINE HOW IT WORKED. FOR EXAMPLE, SOME PEOPLE THINK THE "VENTILATION" SHAFTS ALLOWED THE PHARAOH'S SOUL TO REACH THE STARS: ONE OF THEM POINTS TOWARD SIRIUS.

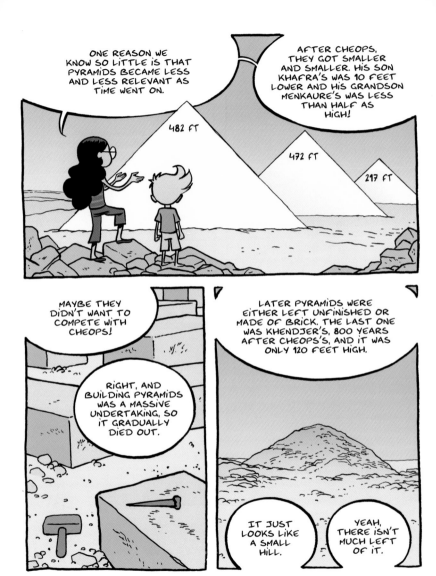

ONE REASON WE KNOW SO LITTLE IS THAT PYRAMIDS BECAME LESS AND LESS RELEVANT AS TIME WENT ON.

AFTER CHEOPS, THEY GOT SMALLER AND SMALLER. HIS SON KHAFRA'S WAS 10 FEET LOWER AND HIS GRANDSON MENKAURE'S WAS LESS THAN HALF AS HIGH!

482 FT

472 FT

217 FT

MAYBE THEY DIDN'T WANT TO COMPETE WITH CHEOPS!

RIGHT, AND BUILDING PYRAMIDS WAS A MASSIVE UNDERTAKING, SO IT GRADUALLY DIED OUT.

LATER PYRAMIDS WERE EITHER LEFT UNFINISHED OR MADE OF BRICK. THE LAST ONE WAS KHENDJER'S, 800 YEARS AFTER CHEOPS'S, AND IT WAS ONLY 120 FEET HIGH.

IT JUST LOOKS LIKE A SMALL HILL.

YEAH, THERE ISN'T MUCH LEFT OF IT.

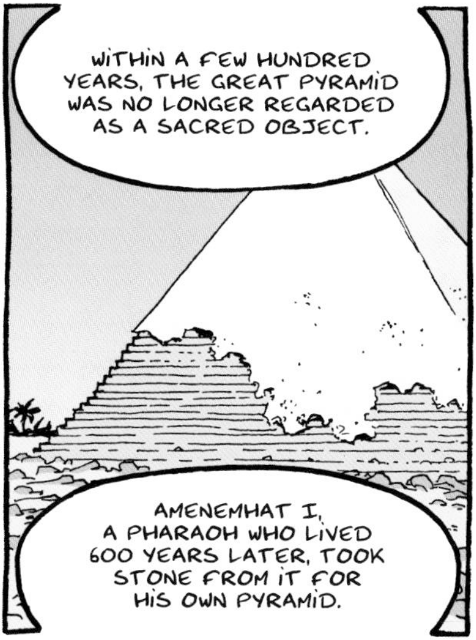
WITHIN A FEW HUNDRED YEARS, THE GREAT PYRAMID WAS NO LONGER REGARDED AS A SACRED OBJECT.
AMENEMHAT I, A PHARAOH WHO LIVED 600 YEARS LATER, TOOK STONE FROM IT FOR HIS OWN PYRAMID.

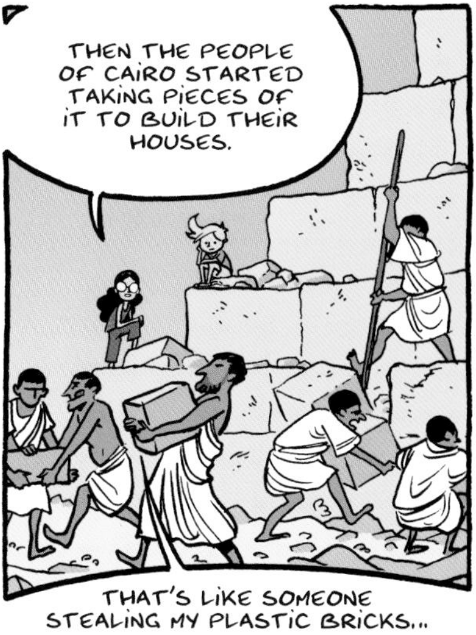
THEN THE PEOPLE OF CAIRO STARTED TAKING PIECES OF IT TO BUILD THEIR HOUSES.
THAT'S LIKE SOMEONE STEALING MY PLASTIC BRICKS...

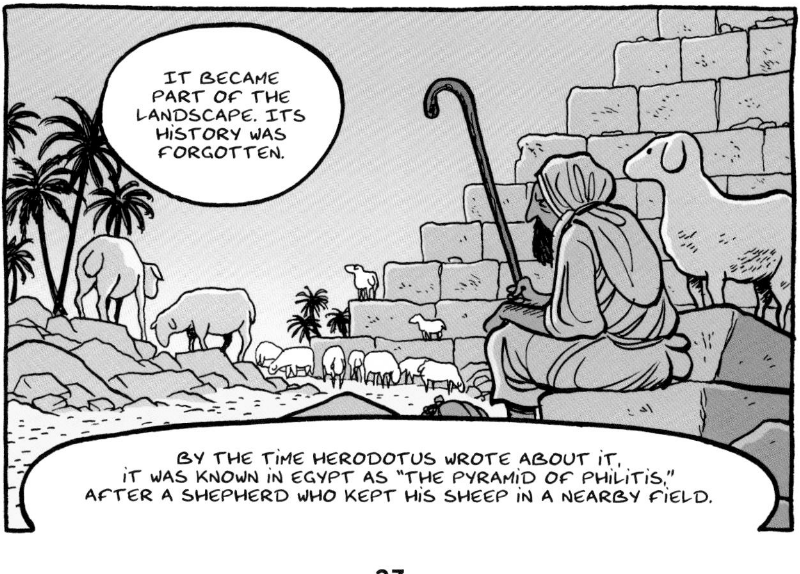
IT BECAME PART OF THE LANDSCAPE. ITS HISTORY WAS FORGOTTEN.
BY THE TIME HERODOTUS WROTE ABOUT IT, IT WAS KNOWN IN EGYPT AS "THE PYRAMID OF PHILITIS," AFTER A SHEPHERD WHO KEPT HIS SHEEP IN A NEARBY FIELD.

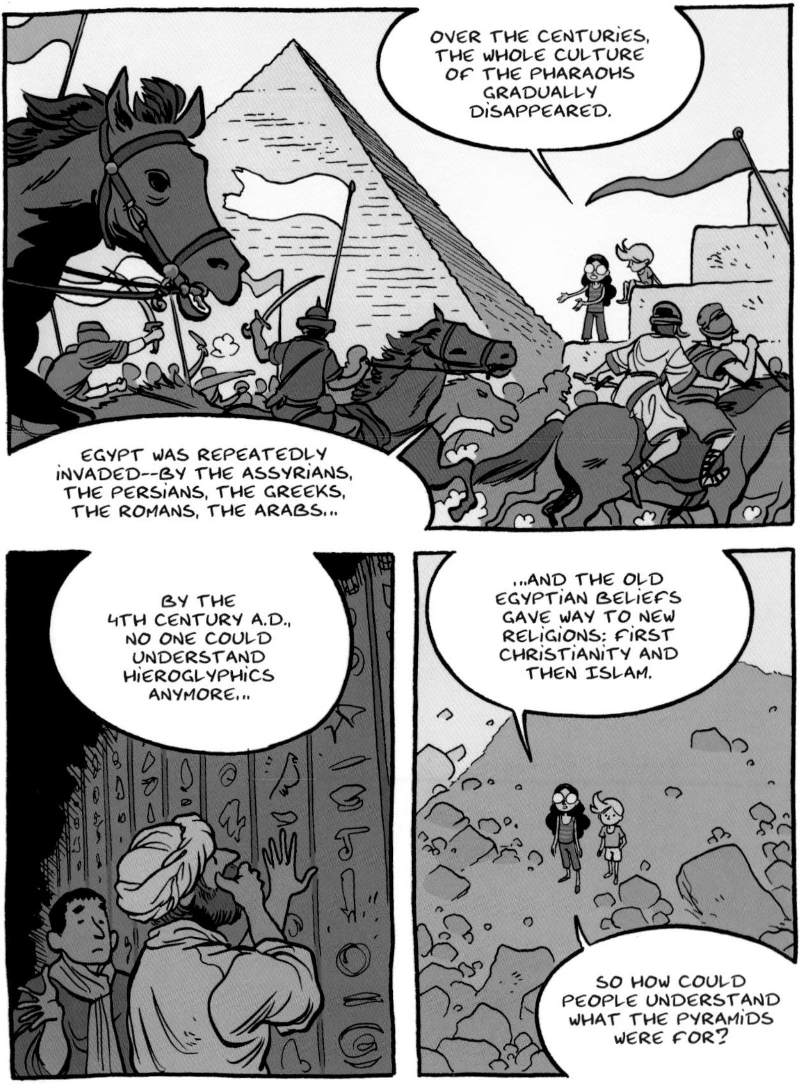
OVER THE CENTURIES, THE WHOLE CULTURE OF THE PHARAOHS GRADUALLY DISAPPEARED.
EGYPT WAS REPEATEDLY INVADED--BY THE ASSYRIANS, THE PERSIANS, THE GREEKS, THE ROMANS, THE ARABS...
BY THE 4TH CENTURY A.D., NO ONE COULD UNDERSTAND HIEROGLYPHICS ANYMORE...
...AND THE OLD EGYPTIAN BELIEFS GAVE WAY TO NEW RELIGIONS: FIRST CHRISTIANITY AND THEN ISLAM.
SO HOW COULD PEOPLE UNDERSTAND WHAT THE PYRAMIDS WERE FOR?

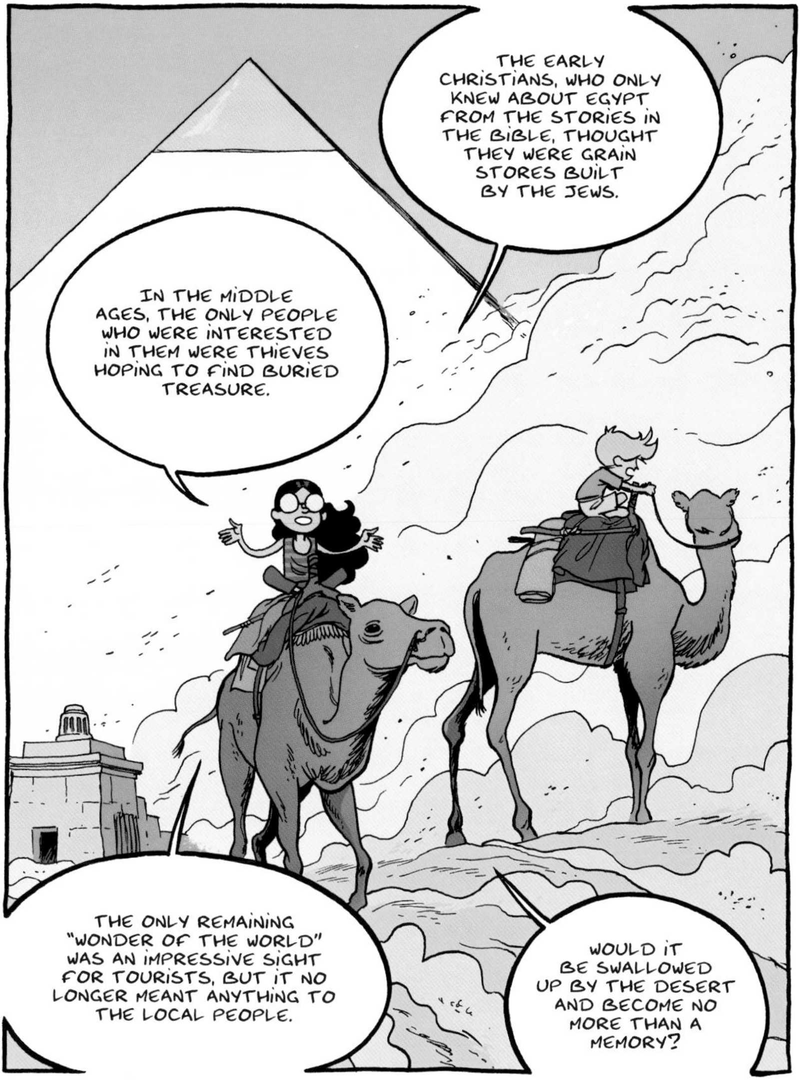
THE EARLY CHRISTIANS, WHO ONLY KNEW ABOUT EGYPT FROM THE STORIES IN THE BIBLE, THOUGHT THEY WERE GRAIN STORES BUILT BY THE JEWS.
IN THE MIDDLE AGES, THE ONLY PEOPLE WHO WERE INTERESTED IN THEM WERE THIEVES HOPING TO FIND BURIED TREASURE.
THE ONLY REMAINING "WONDER OF THE WORLD" WAS AN IMPRESSIVE SIGHT FOR TOURISTS, BUT IT NO LONGER MEANT ANYTHING TO THE LOCAL PEOPLE.
WOULD IT BE SWALLOWED UP BY THE DESERT AND BECOME NO MORE THAN A MEMORY?

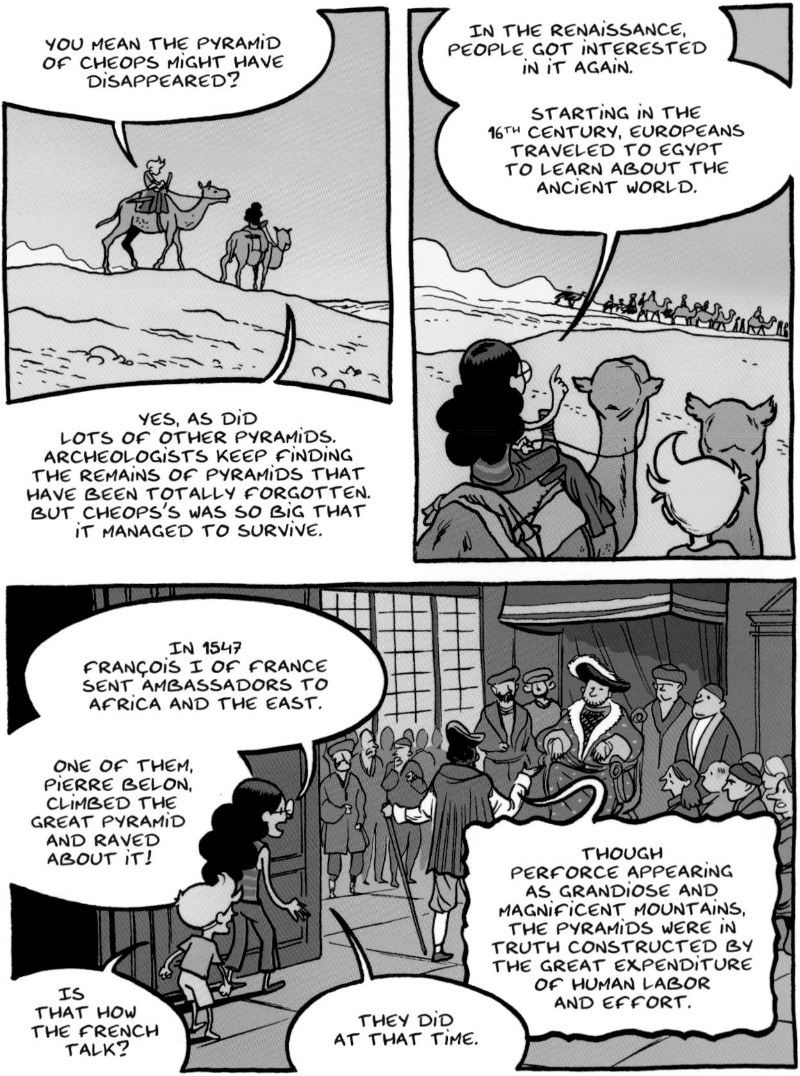
YOU MEAN THE PYRAMID OF CHEOPS MIGHT HAVE DISAPPEARED?
YES, AS DID LOTS OF OTHER PYRAMIDS. ARCHEOLOGISTS KEEP FINDING THE REMAINS OF PYRAMIDS THAT HAVE BEEN TOTALLY FORGOTTEN. BUT CHEOPS'S WAS SO BIG THAT IT MANAGED TO SURVIVE.
IN THE RENAISSANCE, PEOPLE GOT INTERESTED IN IT AGAIN.
STARTING IN THE 16TH CENTURY, EUROPEANS TRAVELED TO EGYPT TO LEARN ABOUT THE ANCIENT WORLD.
IN 1547 FRANÇOIS I OF FRANCE SENT AMBASSADORS TO AFRICA AND THE EAST.
ONE OF THEM, PIERRE BELON, CLIMBED THE GREAT PYRAMID AND RAVED ABOUT IT!
THOUGH PERFORCE APPEARING AS GRANDIOSE AND MAGNIFICENT MOUNTAINS, THE PYRAMIDS WERE IN TRUTH CONSTRUCTED BY THE GREAT EXPENDITURE OF HUMAN LABOR AND EFFORT.
IS THAT HOW THE FRENCH TALK?
THEY DID AT THAT TIME.

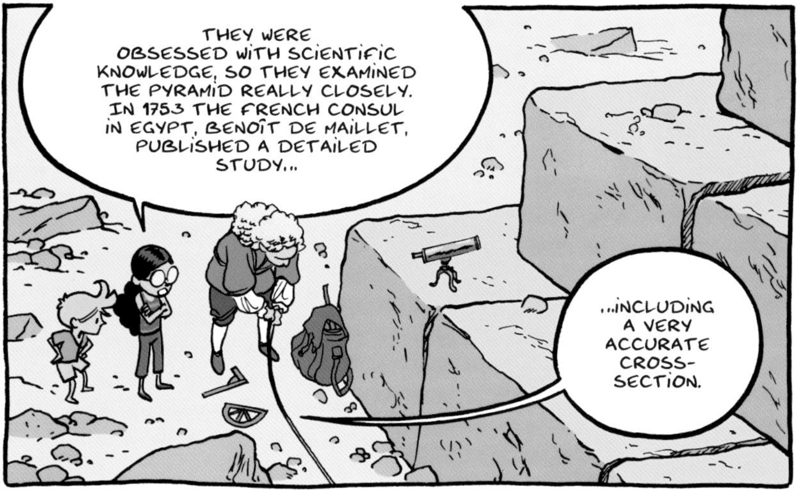
THEY WERE OBSESSED WITH SCIENTIFIC KNOWLEDGE, SO THEY EXAMINED THE PYRAMID REALLY CLOSELY. IN 1753 THE FRENCH CONSUL IN EGYPT, BENOÎT DE MAILLET, PUBLISHED A DETAILED STUDY...
...INCLUDING A VERY ACCURATE CROSS-SECTION.

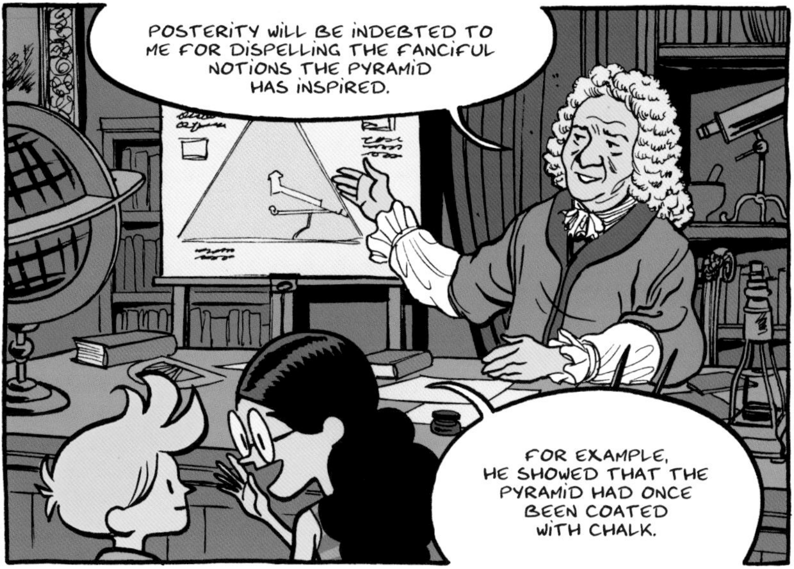
POSTERITY WILL BE INDEBTED TO ME FOR DISPELLING THE FANCIFUL NOTIONS THE PYRAMID HAS INSPIRED.
FOR EXAMPLE, HE SHOWED THAT THE PYRAMID HAD ONCE BEEN COATED WITH CHALK.

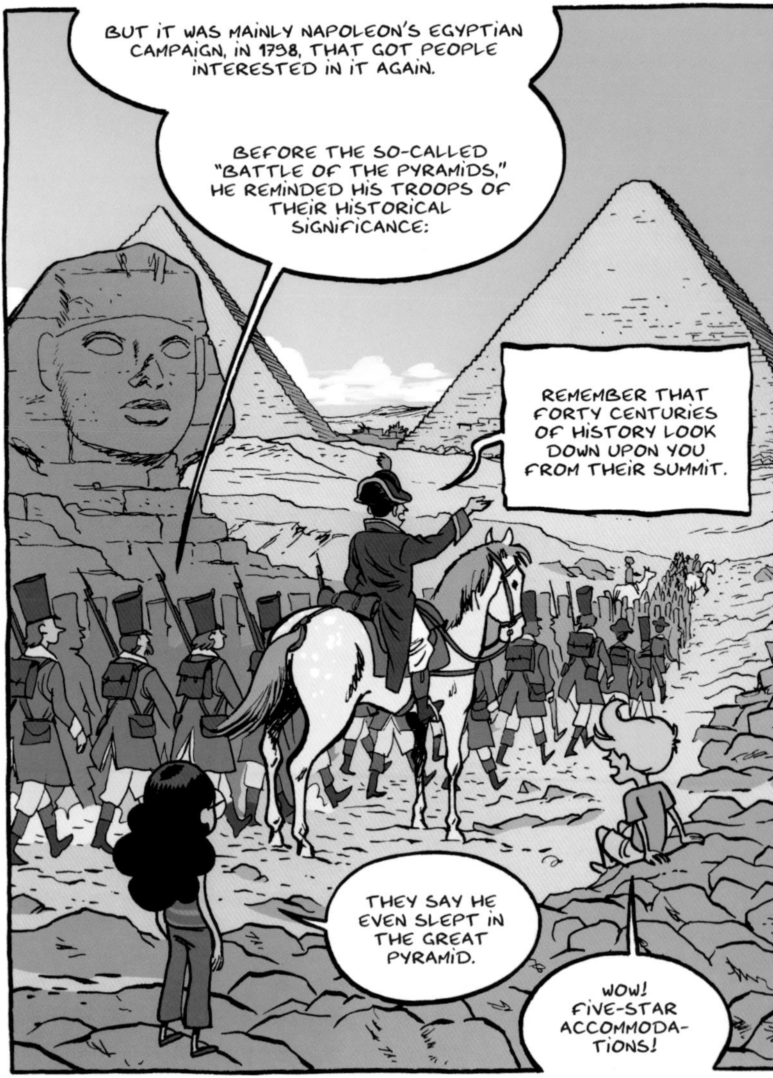
BUT IT WAS MAINLY NAPOLEON'S EGYPTIAN CAMPAIGN, IN 1798, THAT GOT PEOPLE INTERESTED IN IT AGAIN.
BEFORE THE SO-CALLED "BATTLE OF THE PYRAMIDS," HE REMINDED HIS TROOPS OF THEIR HISTORICAL SIGNIFICANCE:
REMEMBER THAT FORTY CENTURIES OF HISTORY LOOK DOWN UPON YOU FROM THEIR SUMMIT.
THEY SAY HE EVEN SLEPT IN THE GREAT PYRAMID.
WOW! FIVE-STAR ACCOMMODA-TIONS!

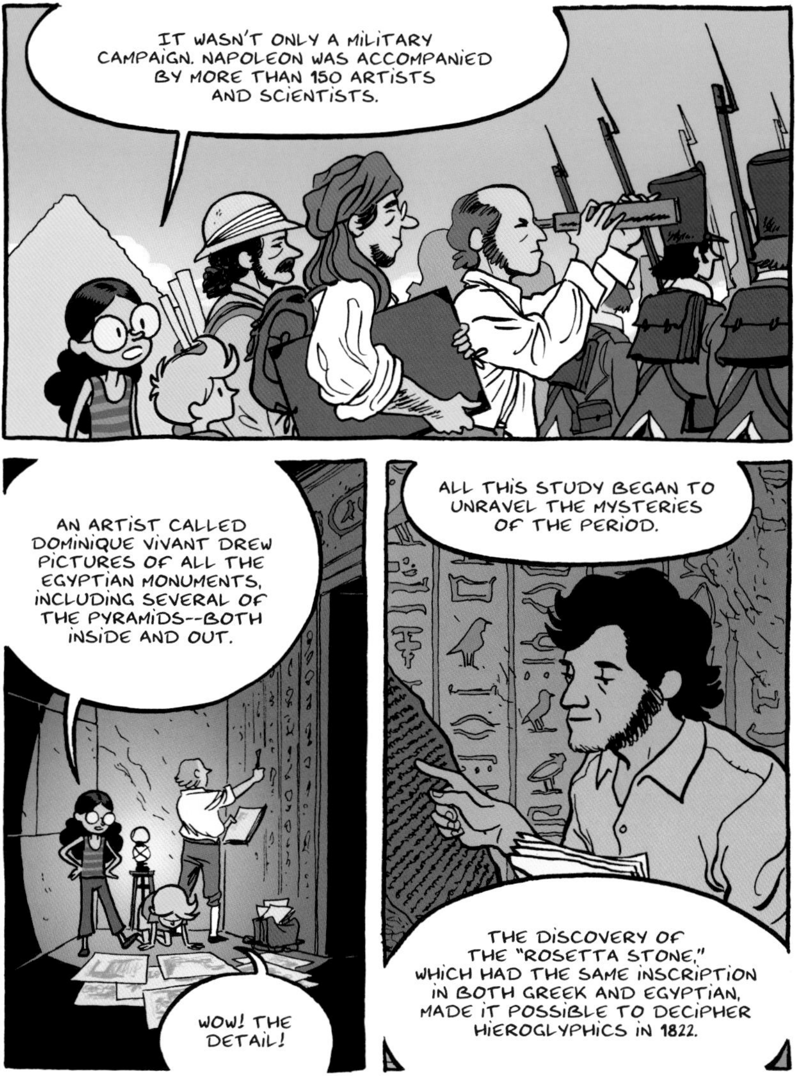
IT WASN'T ONLY A MILITARY CAMPAIGN. NAPOLEON WAS ACCOMPANIED BY MORE THAN 150 ARTISTS AND SCIENTISTS.
AN ARTIST CALLED DOMINIQUE VIVANT DREW PICTURES OF ALL THE EGYPTIAN MONUMENTS, INCLUDING SEVERAL OF THE PYRAMIDS--BOTH INSIDE AND OUT.
WOW! THE DETAIL!
ALL THIS STUDY BEGAN TO UNRAVEL THE MYSTERIES OF THE PERIOD.
THE DISCOVERY OF THE "ROSETTA STONE," WHICH HAD THE SAME INSCRIPTION IN BOTH GREEK AND EGYPTIAN, MADE IT POSSIBLE TO DECIPHER HIEROGLYPHICS IN 1822.

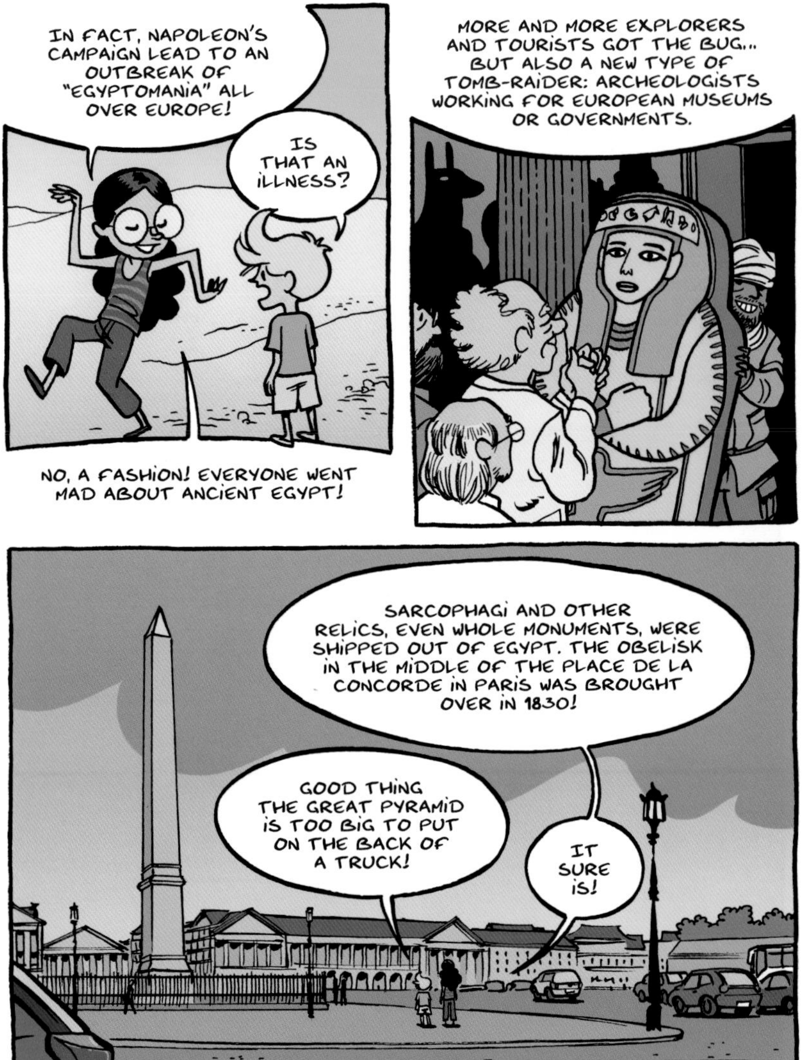
IN FACT, NAPOLEON'S CAMPAIGN LEAD TO AN OUTBREAK OF "EGYPTOMANIA" ALL OVER EUROPE!
IS THAT AN ILLNESS?
NO, A FASHION! EVERYONE WENT MAD ABOUT ANCIENT EGYPT!
MORE AND MORE EXPLORERS AND TOURISTS GOT THE BUG... BUT ALSO A NEW TYPE OF TOMB-RAIDER: ARCHEOLOGISTS WORKING FOR EUROPEAN MUSEUMS OR GOVERNMENTS.
SARCOPHAGI AND OTHER RELICS, EVEN WHOLE MONUMENTS, WERE SHIPPED OUT OF EGYPT. THE OBELISK IN THE MIDDLE OF THE PLACE DE LA CONCORDE IN PARIS WAS BROUGHT OVER IN 1830!
GOOD THING THE GREAT PYRAMID IS TOO BIG TO PUT ON THE BACK OF A TRUCK!
IT SURE IS!

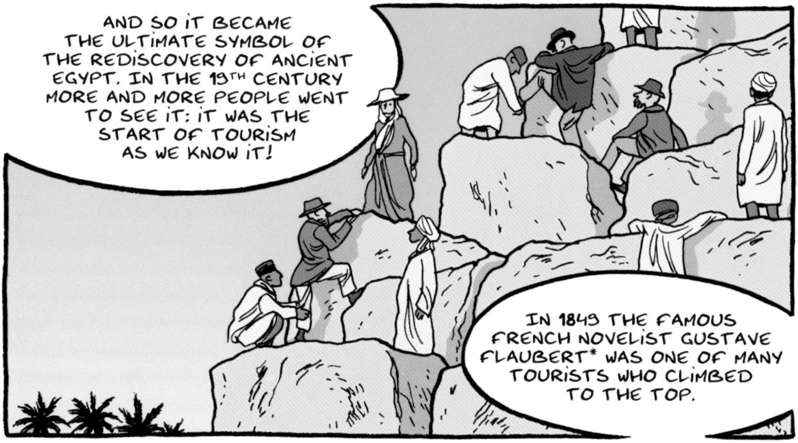
AND SO IT BECAME THE ULTIMATE SYMBOL OF THE REDISCOVERY OF ANCIENT EGYPT. IN THE 19TH CENTURY MORE AND MORE PEOPLE WENT TO SEE IT: IT WAS THE START OF TOURISM AS WE KNOW IT!
IN 1849 THE FAMOUS FRENCH NOVELIST GUSTAVE FLAUBERT* WAS ONE OF MANY TOURISTS WHO CLIMBED TO THE TOP.

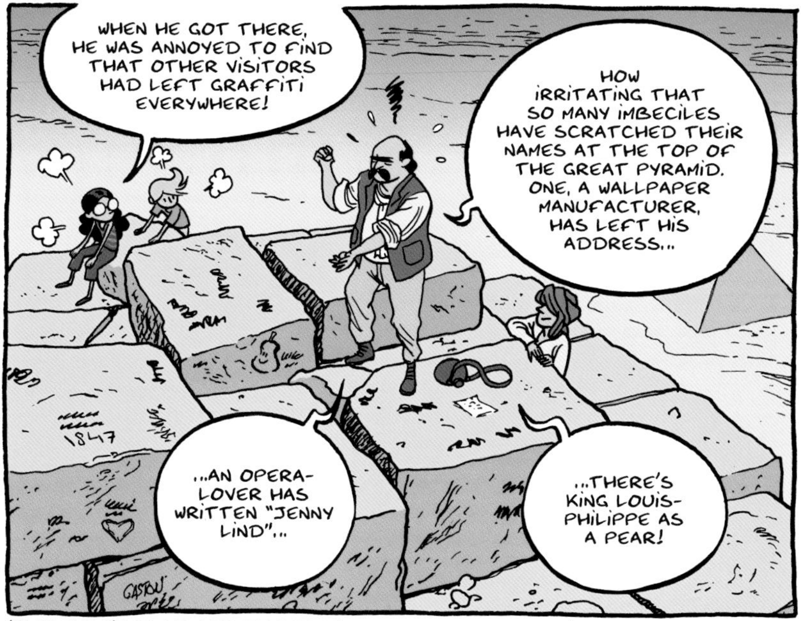
WHEN HE GOT THERE, HE WAS ANNOYED TO FIND THAT OTHER VISITORS HAD LEFT GRAFFITI EVERYWHERE!
HOW IRRITATING THAT SO MANY IMBECILES HAVE SCRATCHED THEIR NAMES AT THE TOP OF THE GREAT PYRAMID. ONE, A WALLPAPER MANUFACTURER, HAS LEFT HIS ADDRESS...
...AN OPERA-LOVER HAS WRITTEN "JENNY LIND"...
...THERE'S KING LOUIS-PHILIPPE AS A PEAR!
1847
GASTON

("OVER THE FIELDS AND OVER THE SHORES" BY GUSTAVE FLAUBERT, 1886.)

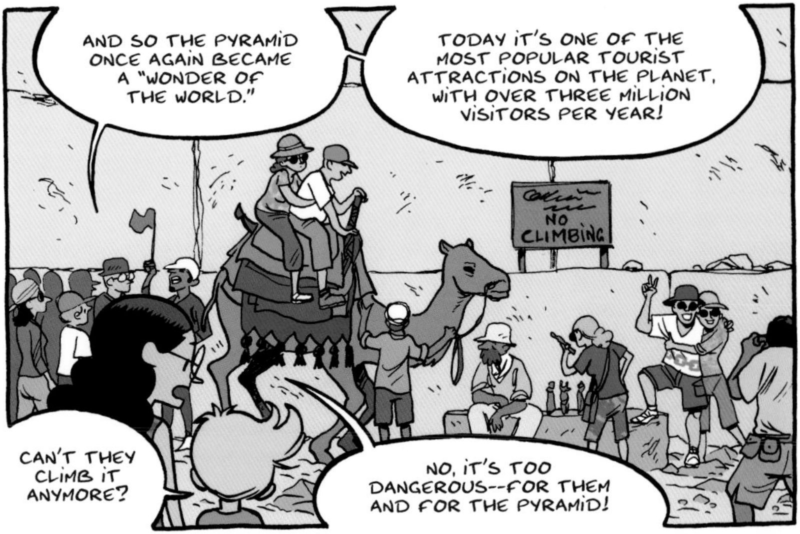
AND SO THE PYRAMID ONCE AGAIN BECAME A "WONDER OF THE WORLD."
TODAY IT'S ONE OF THE MOST POPULAR TOURIST ATTRACTIONS ON THE PLANET, WITH OVER THREE MILLION VISITORS PER YEAR!
NO CLIMBING
CAN'T THEY CLIMB IT ANYMORE?
NO, IT'S TOO DANGEROUS--FOR THEM AND FOR THE PYRAMID!

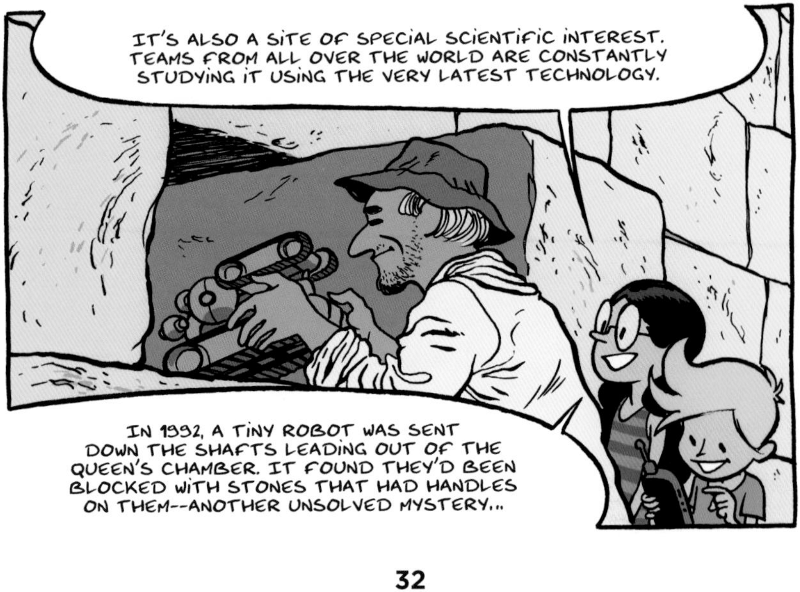
IT'S ALSO A SITE OF SPECIAL SCIENTIFIC INTEREST. TEAMS FROM ALL OVER THE WORLD ARE CONSTANTLY STUDYING IT USING THE VERY LATEST TECHNOLOGY.
IN 1992, A TINY ROBOT WAS SENT DOWN THE SHAFTS LEADING OUT OF THE QUEEN'S CHAMBER. IT FOUND THEY'D BEEN BLOCKED WITH STONES THAT HAD HANDLES ON THEM--ANOTHER UNSOLVED MYSTERY...

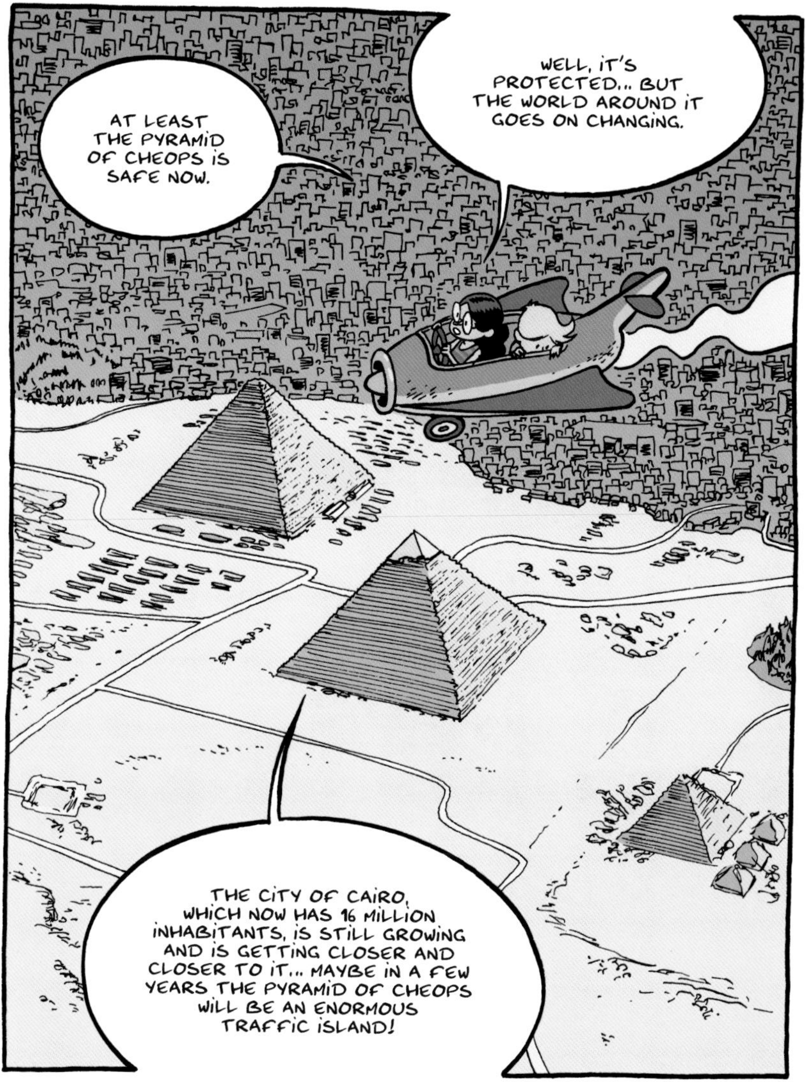
AT LEAST THE PYRAMID OF CHEOPS IS SAFE NOW.
WELL, IT'S PROTECTED... BUT THE WORLD AROUND IT GOES ON CHANGING.
THE CITY OF CAIRO, WHICH NOW HAS 16 MILLION INHABITANTS, IS STILL GROWING AND IS GETTING CLOSER AND CLOSER TO IT... MAYBE IN A FEW YEARS THE PYRAMID OF CHEOPS WILL BE AN ENORMOUS TRAFFIC ISLAND!

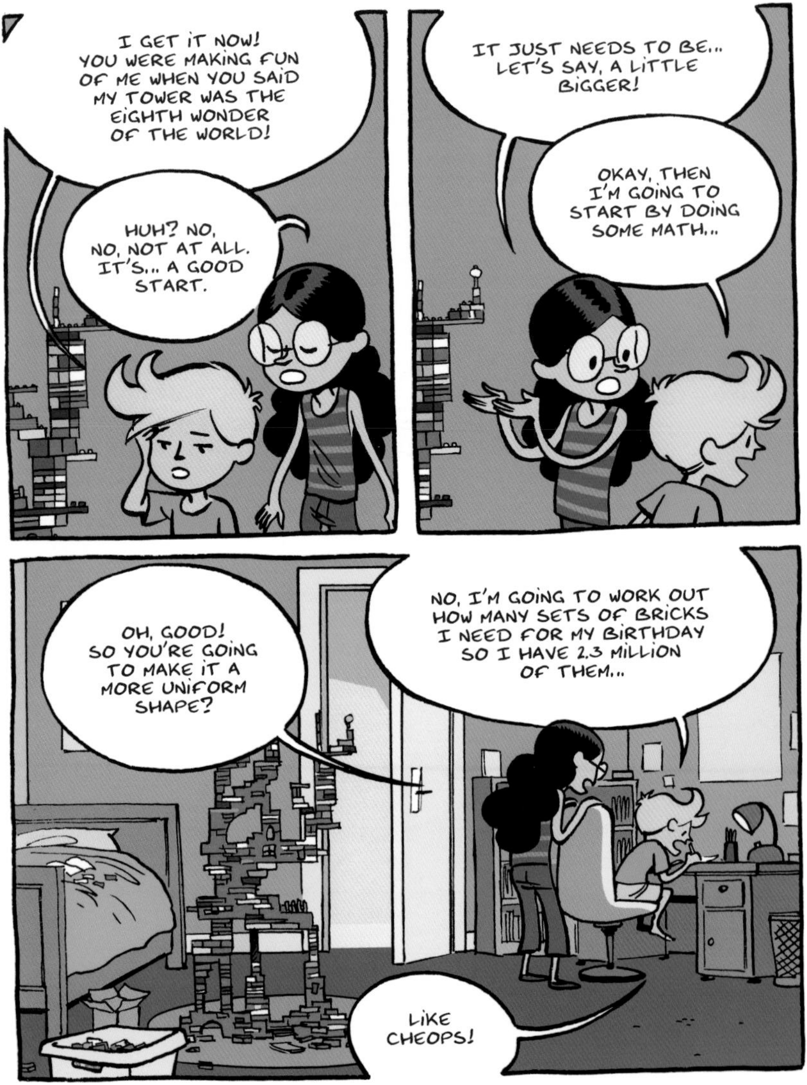
I GET IT NOW! YOU WERE MAKING FUN OF ME WHEN YOU SAID MY TOWER WAS THE EIGHTH WONDER OF THE WORLD!
HUH? NO, NO, NOT AT ALL. IT'S... A GOOD START.
IT JUST NEEDS TO BE... LET'S SAY, A LITTLE BIGGER!
OKAY, THEN I'M GOING TO START BY DOING SOME MATH...
OH, GOOD! SO YOU'RE GOING TO MAKE IT A MORE UNIFORM SHAPE?
NO, I'M GOING TO WORK OUT HOW MANY SETS OF BRICKS I NEED FOR MY BIRTHDAY SO I HAVE 2.3 MILLION OF THEM...
LIKE CHEOPS!

And there's more...

Some people who made history

Cheops
(c. 2500 B.C.)

Cheops was one of the 4th Dynasty of pharaohs. Despite his legacy of vast buildings, very little is known about him. He probably ruled for 22 to 40 years in the early 17th century B.C. Cheops (or Khêops) was his Greek name, and he's also known by his Egyptian name Khufu, and as Súphis, Sofe, Saurid, and Salhuk.

Imhotep
(c. 3000 B.C.)

Imhotep was a doctor, architect, and philosopher, and he was Pharaoh Djoser's vizier (personal advisor). He designed the pharaoh's tomb as a stepped pyramid, which was the first type of pyramid to be built. He was made a god after his death.

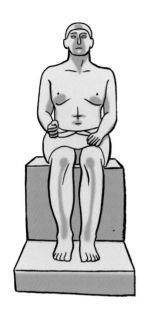

Hemiunu
(c. 2500 B.C.)

A grandson of Pharaoh Sneferu, Hemiunu was Cheops's vizir and the designer of the Great Pyramid. He also built himself a mastaba (tomb), which was discovered by archeologists in the early 20th century, along with an almost perfectly preserved statue of him.

Herodotus
(born 480 B.C., died c. 425 B.C.)

A Greek explorer known as "The Father of History," Herodotus talked to people living around the Mediterranean and wrote about them in *The Histories,* a work that became a key source of information about the ancient world—and about Cheops and the pyramids—right up until modern times.

The Giza Plateau

The Giza Pyramids stand on a chalk plateau that was leveled for the purpose. They each have one side facing north, one facing south, one facing east and one facing west.

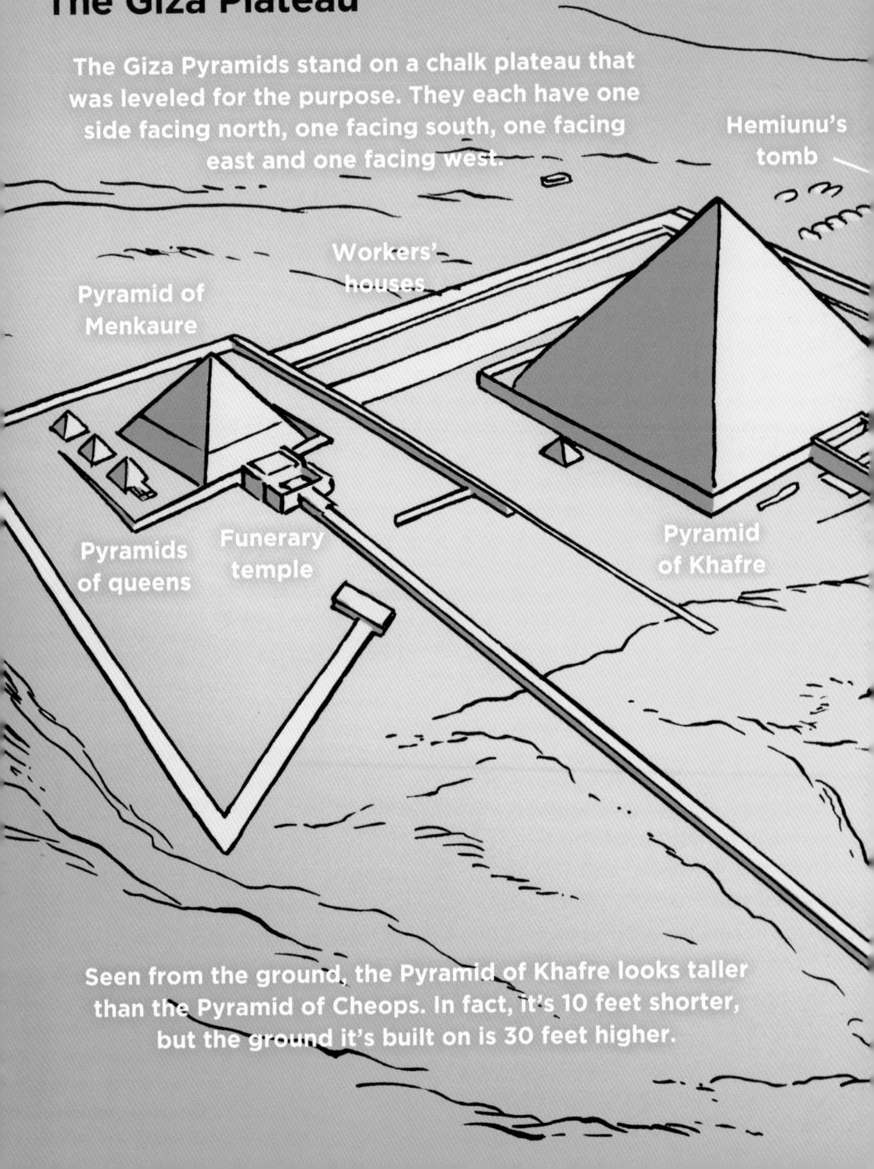

Hemiunu's tomb
Workers' houses
Pyramid of Menkaure
Pyramids of queens
Funerary temple
Pyramid of Khafre

Seen from the ground, the Pyramid of Khafre looks taller than the Pyramid of Cheops. In fact, it's 10 feet shorter, but the ground it's built on is 30 feet higher.

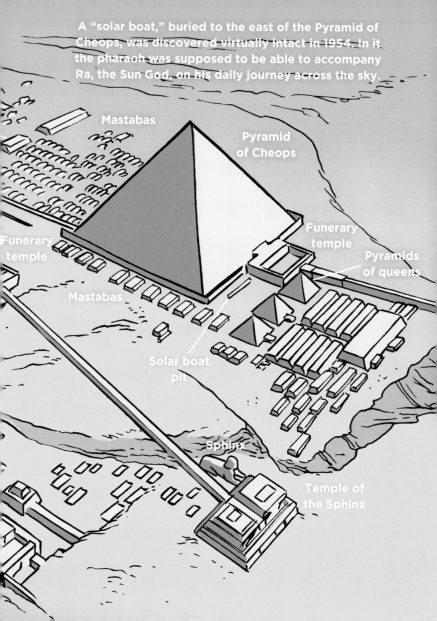

A "solar boat," buried to the east of the Pyramid of Cheops, was discovered virtually intact in 1954. In it the pharaoh was supposed to be able to accompany Ra, the Sun God, on his daily journey across the sky.

Mastabas

Pyramid of Cheops

Funerary temple

Funerary temple

Pyramids of queens

Mastabas

Solar boat pit

Sphinx

Temple of the Sphinx

The six other Wonders of the World

The Hanging Gardens of Babylon

According to legend, King Nebuchadnezzar II had magnificent terraced gardens built around 600 B.C. in the city of Babylon, in what is now part of Iraq, but archeologists have found no trace of their existence.

The Statue of Zeus at Olympia

An ivory and gold statue of the King of the Gods was carved by Phidias around 436 B.C. It was moved from Olympia (in Greece) to Constantinople (now Istanbul) 800 years later and was destroyed by fire.

The Temple of Artemis at Ephesus

The Greek king Croesus had this vast temple (over 425 feet long) built at Ephesus in 560 B.C., but it was burned to the ground in 356 B.C. by a man who hoped this would make him famous.

The Mausoleum at Halicarnassus

A giant tomb, more than 160 feet high, built for Mausolus, a Persian King, in 353 B.C. at Halicarnassus— now Bodrum in Turkey. It collapsed in the Middle Ages and is now a ruin.

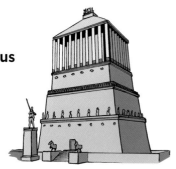

The Colossus of Rhodes

An enormous bronze statue (over 100 feet high) of Helios, the Sun God, was built around 292 B.C. at the entrance to the Greek port of Rhodes. It was destroyed by an earthquake 65 years later.

The Lighthouse of Alexandria

Built around 290 B.C., the lighthouse, which was visible from a distance of 30 miles, was used by sailors for 1,700 years. It was destroyed by a succession of earthquakes.

Timeline

Imhotep designs the first pyramid for Pharaoh Djoser.
▼

2650 B.C.

Pharaoh Sneferu, Cheops's father, makes several attempts at building a smooth pyramid, finally succeeding with "The Red Pyramid."
▼

2590–2560 B.C.

0

450 B.C.

1550 B.C.

▲
The Greek historian Herodotus visits Egypt and collects information about Cheops.

▲
Ahmose builds the last pyramid.

820 A.D.

1500–1700 A.D.

▲
Khalif Al-Ma'mun breaks open the north face of the Pyramid of Cheops.

▲
European explorers rediscover the Egyptian pyramids.

Cheops builds the Great
Pyramid on the Giza Plateau,
15 miles from Cairo.
▼

The Pyramids of Khafre
and Menkaure complete
the Giza site.
▼

**2580–2560
B.C.**

**2570-2510
B.C.**

**1991–1962
B.C.**

**2500–2300
B.C.**

▲
During his reign, Amenemhat I
uses stones from the Pyramid
of Cheops to build his own
memorial complex.

▲
Pharaohs build their
pyramids at another
site, Abusir.

**1798
A.D.**

**1979
A.D.**

▲
Napoleon Bonaparte wins
"The Battle of the Pyramids,"
part of his Egyptian campaign.

▲
The Pyramids of Giza
become a UNESCO
World Heritage Site.

WATCH OUT FOR PAPERCUTZ

Welcome to premiere volume of MAGICAL HISTORY TOUR #1 "The Great Pyramid," by Fabrice Erre and Sylvain Savoia, from Papercutz, those fun-loving folks dedicated to publishing great graphic novels for all ages. I'm Jim Salicrup, the Editor-in-Chief and your tour guide through the wonders of Papercutz.

All-new, full-color Graphic Novel
Geronimo Stilton
THE SECRET OF THE SPHINX
PAPERCUTZ

Papercutz has visited the Great Pyramids twice before. First in GERONIMO STILTON #2 "The Secret of the Sphinx." Geronimo's the editor of *The Rodent's Gazette*, and he often travels through time to save the future, by protecting the past. Even though Geronimo's world is sort of a mousified version of our own, and the story is mostly about the Sphinx, the first thing Geronimo sees back in ancient Egypt is the pyramid of Cheops.

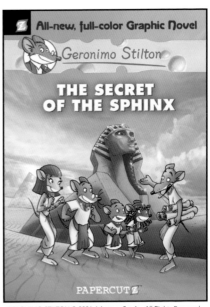

More recently, Papercutz has published ASTERIX, the international bestselling adventures of two Gauls, Asterix and Obelix, who defend their tiny village from being conquered by the Roman Empire back in 50 BC. Their secret weapon—a magic potion that gives them super-strength. In ASTERIX Volume Two, our heroes journey to Egypt to help Cleopatra win a bet she made with Julius Caesar. While this story reveals a secret of the Sphinx you won't find in any history books, you also get to see Asterix and Obelix explore a great pyramid.

But the MAGICAL HISTORY TOUR is not over yet! It's just beginning, available now at booksellers and libraries is MAGICAL HISTORY TOUR #2 "The Great Wall of China." Join Annie and Nico as they explore and discover fascinating facts about the most famous wall of all (that's still standing)!

Thanks,
Jim

THE INTERNATIONAL BESTSELLER
R. GOSCINNY
A. UDERZO
ASTERIX
FEATURING 3 CLASSIC GRAPHIC NOVELS IN 1
ASTERIX THE GLADIATOR
ASTERIX AND THE BANQUET
ASTERIX AND CLEOPATRA
PAPERCUT

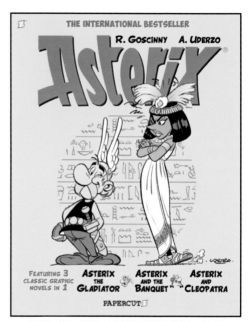

STAY IN TOUCH!

EMAIL:	salicrup@papercutz.com
WEB:	www.papercutz.com
TWITTER:	@papercutzgn
FACEBOOK:	PAPERCUTZGRAPHICNOVELS
REGULAR MAIL:	Papercutz, 160 Broadway, Suite 700, East Wing, New York, NY 10038

Fabrice Erre has a Ph.D. in History and teaches Geography and History at the Lycee Jean Jaures near Montpellier, France. He has written a thesis on the satirical press, writes the blog *Une annee au lycee (A Year in High School)* on the website of *Le Monde*, one of France's top national newspapers, and has published several comics.

Sylvain Savoia draws the *Marzi* series, which tells the history of Poland as seen through the eyes of a child. He has also drawn *Les esclaves oublies de Tromelin (The Forgotten Slaves of Tromelin)*, which won the Academie de Marine de Paris prize.